C000125757

Heart *of the* Holy Land

40 Reflections on Scripture and Place

Paul H. Wright

ROSE PUBLISHING

Heart of the Holy Land: 40 Reflections on Scripture and Place

Copyright © 2020 Paul H. Wright
Published by Rose Publishing
An imprint of Hendrickson Publishing Group
Rose Publishing, LLC
P.O. Box 3473
Peabody, Massachusetts 01961-3473 USA
www.hendricksonpublishinggroup.com

ISBN 978-1-62862-840-1

All rights reserved. No part of this work may be reproduced or transmitted in any form or by any means, electronic or mechanical, including photocopying, recording, or by any information storage and retrieval system, without permission in writing from the publisher.

Scripture quotations taken from the New American Standard Bible® (NASB), Copyright © 1960, 1962, 1963, 1968, 1971, 1972, 1973, 1975, 1977, 1995 by The Lockman Foundation. Used by permission. www.Lockman.org

Book cover and page design by Sergio Urquiza.

Printed in the United States of America
010720VP

Contents

To Diane, with signposts of our shared journey.

Getting Ready

This book is about an ongoing journey—your journey, and mine as well. Its setting is the Holy Land, where my wife and I have been privileged to live for nearly a quarter century, time enough to learn to hear its heartbeat and sense its call to life. The name Holy Land is descriptive, but also handy. It's descriptive because it speaks of a "God-trodden land." The phrase "God-trodden land" comes from a pilgrim's inscription found in ancient Amaseia in Pontus, now north-central Turkey, which mentions places where God became imminent—present—to the men and women of the Bible. And it's handy because it is a single term that embraces not only the land of ancient Israel but the lands of Israel's near neighbors as well. Ammon, Moab, Edom, and the wilderness of Sinai were also scenes of activity in the biblical story. Today these lands fall within the borders of several countries: the modern state of Israel with the Palestinian territories, the Hashemite Kingdom of Jordan, and the Arab Republic of Egypt. Together, they claim the title "lands of the Bible."

The focus of our shared journey is the Dan to Beersheba heartland of the biblical story, with Jerusalem the center. To here is the inward journey of Abraham; from here the outward journeys of the apostles. Whether you've been to the Holy Land or not, you already roam the land vicariously whenever you read the Bible, a book that is immersed in the landscape of ancient Israel, jam-packed with geographical language and imagery. But if you have already come, you've also encountered it personally and embraced something of its living reality—its storied landscapes; actual remains, now excavated, from Bible times; and people whose ancestral roots in these lands reach back hundreds if not thousands of years.

I often hear the claim, "When I visited the Holy Land, the Bible came alive!" That discovery is palpable, but not exactly accurate: according to Hebrews 4:12, the Bible *already is* alive, "living and active." What happens is that we become more alive to it, more aware of its texture, its color, its feel, and its tug. The reality has been there all along; we are the ones who have moved (see Isa. 40:8; 55:11). Like the apostle John, we become eyewitnesses for having heard and seen and beheld realities "concerning the Word of Life" (1 John 1:1).

On these pages you will find forty reflections on the Holy Land. Each one weaves a biblical or modern event into the landed context in which it took place. These are places that you, too, can explore on your trip to the Holy Land. But you don't actually have to be in the land to benefit, since each also touches aspects of real life—your life, my life, the lives of people we know—that are common to our experiences wherever we live.

The reflections are organized by place, starting with introductory topics such as climate, roads, and the fertility of the land. Then they zero in on Jerusalem, the highpoint for most visitors to the lands of the Bible. From Jerusalem, they will lead you down to Jericho and the Dead Sea, into the southern desert, all the way to Mount Sinai, up into Galilee, out to the Mediterranean coast, and over to Jordan. Some of the sites that you will encounter on your journey through these pages are common to normal Holy Land tour itineraries. Besides Jerusalem, I include, for instance, Caesarea, Nazareth, the Sea of Galilee, Dan, Megiddo, Jericho, and Bethlehem. Others, such as Mount Gerizim, the Emmaus Road, Jezreel, and Nain, are a bit off-road (off the typical modern tour route, that is, not the ancient network of highways). And so I have set signposts at the start of each reflection to point you to places that will help you organize your own Bible reading or travel through the Holy Land. Here and there, I provide tools to aid your reading and deepen your Bible study as well.

Let's borrow the words of Moses, spoken in encouragement as he and all Israel stood on the plains of Moab east of the Jordan River, gazing into the land of promise: "See, I have placed the land before you; go in ..." (Deut. 1:8). We'll take the journey together.

Mount Zion, Jerusalem

September 2019

1. Reading the Bible with Geographical Eyes

As serious Bible readers, we want to know God better. It's an awesome thought, really, that the all-powerful creator of the universe chose to reveal himself to the people who inhabit Planet Earth, a speck in the vast darkness of space. The Bible tells us how God entered the world of flesh and blood—our world, although in a time long ago and a place far away from where most of us live—in order to redeem people. Over the course of centuries, we read, God spoke to a small band of eager yet stubborn peo-

ple who clung to a narrow land hugging the southeastern shore of the Mediterranean. Abraham, Rachel, Moses, Ruth, David, Isaiah, Mary, Anna—all sentinels of the past who marked God's words well, but who also looked to what the apostle Paul called "the fullness of the time" (Gal. 4:4) when, in the fullness of place, God would dirty his hands and feet in a small, noisy, and very needy corner of the Roman Empire called Galilee.

Unlike the sacred books of many of the world's other great religions, the Bible is full of stories of real people living in real places at real times. God's decision to communicate eternal truth through fallible human

The Sea of Galilee from the hills above Capernaum.

Harvest time in Galilee. As Jesus "kept increasing in wisdom and stature" (Luke 2:52), he walked through fields such as these, picking up imagery he would later use in parables.

beings, to wrap his message around people's experiences with rock and soil and water, is both mind-boggling and humbling. It also suggests that we can better understand God's revelation to us if we take the time to learn about and appreciate the physical contexts in which it was given.

The writers of the Bible knew the land in which God chose to reveal himself well. It was, after all, their home. They were intimately familiar with the rugged terrain of Judah, with cold winter rain and scorching desert heat. They had experienced the relief offered by a small spring of water or the shelter of a crevasse in a mighty rock. They knew what it meant for the hills surrounding their city or village to be filled with enemies, or to lie down securely at night after a full harvest. Time and again, the Bible's historians, prophets, and poets infused the divine message they had to tell with geographical information. In fact, such information fills the biblical text—and its authors assumed their readers knew even more.

By carefully studying the geographical settings of the Bible, we are able to enter more deeply into its world. It becomes possible to follow Joshua's army into the hill country of Canaan (Josh. 6–11), or to crest the hill on which David's Jerusalem stood and experience a bit of the energy of the Songs of Ascents (Pss. 120–134). Jesus must have climbed the hills above Capernaum often in the early mornings to gaze out over the Sea of Galilee (see Mark 1:35). By doing the same today, we can better appreciate Jesus' call to ministry, or our own place in the kingdom of God.

Let's listen to what Jesus said, but also to what he did:

> *He began to teach again by the sea. And such a very large crowd gathered to Him that He got into a boat in the sea and sat down; and the whole crowd was by the sea on the land.*
> *And He was teaching them many things in parables, and was saying to them in His teaching, "Listen to this! Behold, the sower went out to sow . . ."*
>
> —Mark 4:1–3

Joshua entered Canaan from the east, through the wilderness above Jericho (seen here in late winter).

Jesus met people exactly where they were, at a specific place and a specific time. While the eternal truths of the Bible transcend time and place, they are also rooted in it. We are called to live with one eye focused on heaven, the other on the ground—and in this living in between we do well to consider how those who graced the pages of the Bible did the same. It's a fresh adventure, with something new every day.

2. Finding the Good Way

Signposts: Anywhere in Judea, Samaria, or Galilee

Most visitors to Israel today zip along the countryside in air-conditioned motor coaches, largely oblivious to the challenges and adventures that those traveling the land faced in premodern times. Short stops according to prearranged itineraries do little to move a traveler beyond the tourist stage. Rather, it is only by taking time to walk the hills and valleys of Israel, as Jesus did, that we start to get in touch with the world of the Bible.

During biblical times, travelers in the land of Israel faced many obstacles: rough terrain, swampy ground, sand dunes, a lack of adequate drinking water, insufferable heat, sleet

The descent to the oasis of Jericho on the natural route from Jerusalem. This road was paved in the second century AD, and then again only after the First World War.

15

and snow, wind and blowing dust. Added to these was the ever-present danger of brigands and roadside thieves, eagerly awaiting unsuspecting travelers at every turn.

The roads that connected towns and villages in ancient Israel followed natural routes. These routes avoided as many obstacles as possible by following paths of least resistance. For instance, routes into and out of the rugged hill country of Judah tended to follow the tops of ridges rather than dropping into the steep, rocky valleys below. These ridge tops offered a measure of security,

Tracking by camel through Wadi Rum in south Jordan, where the routes are long and water sources few.

and it was here that many towns and villages were located during the biblical period.

For the most part, travel by foot or even donkey cart required that little improvement be made to what were basically donkey paths over hills and through fields. Strong kings would typically improve important roads by cutting brush and clearing stones (see Judg. 5:6–7; Isa. 40:3; 57:14; 62:10). However, most of the time long journeys were nothing short of arduous. An ancient Egyptian document dating to the late thirteenth century BC describes the journey of a traveler who crossed the land of Canaan. The scribe reports that when the traveler halted each night, his crushed and battered body collapsed into sleep.

Eventually, the Romans built a series of improved roads that connected the major cities of Judea, Samaria, and Galilee with the rest of the Roman Empire. In doing so, they graded steep hillsides, built bridges over watercourses, and installed paving, curbing, and milestones. For the most part, these improvements were made in the centuries following the events of New Testament. For this reason, it is not technically correct to say that Jesus walked a Roman road between Jericho and Jerusalem; rather, he walked a natural route that was incorporated into the Roman road system in the following century.

The prophet Jeremiah used the familiar image of journeying through a rugged land to speak about the human heart:

*Thus says the LORD, "Stand by the ways
and see and ask for the ancient paths, where
the good way is, and walk in it; and you
will find rest for your souls."*

—Jeremiah 6:16

Perhaps because difficult travel conditions were such an everyday part of life in the ancient world, the biblical writers never tired of using travel imagery to speak about a larger journey, the journey each of us takes through life (Gen. 17:1; Deut. 8:6; Ps. 119:1, 105; John 14:6; Acts 9:2). Unfortunately, it has become so cliché to speak about "walking with God along life's way" that we rarely pause to reflect on the enormity of the task. Life's journey is seldom easy, and often an arduous experience. Moreover, in the bibli-

Natural routes through the Judean wilderness follow the tops of ridges.

cal record journeys were often high points of faith—one need only recall the travels of Abraham, Moses, Nehemiah, the apostle Paul, and of course Jesus on the way to the cross. It is good to know that as believers in Jesus, we can follow one who has walked life's paths before us, showing us where to step along the way.

3. The Twelve-Inch Line

Perhaps ancient Israel's most familiar label is that it is "a land flowing with milk and honey" (Ex. 3:17; Deut. 11:9; etc.). Here and there the writers of the Bible added additional descriptions: it is "a good and spacious land" (Ex. 3:8), "the Beautiful Land" (Dan. 11:41), "the glory of all lands" (Ezek. 20:6), "a pleasant land, the most beautiful inheritance of the nations" (Jer. 3:19). When we read verses like these, we tend to think of places of great comfort and material blessing, or situations in life that are bounteous and full. But a quick look at the actual landscape of Israel makes us wonder how descriptions like these fit. Much of the land of the Bible is harsh, barren, and bare—the drive from Jerusalem to Jericho for instance, the shoreline along Dead Sea, the shallow Beersheba and Arad basins, or just about anywhere during the long parched heat of summer. "Look," the drifters of the Great Depression said in John Steinbeck's *The Grapes of Wrath* (chapter 20), "this ain't no lan' of milk an' honey like the preachers say ..." Their disenchantment reflects the bewilderment of many visitors to Israel whose actual views of the land are something less than the milk and honey images they came with. The usual explanations for this disparity are three. Compared to forty years of wandering in the Sinai wasteland, anything in Canaan was beautiful to behold (see Ex. 16:3). "Milk and honey" smacks of what someone would nostalgically say about any home they have been away from too long. Or, the land actually does have potential—it only needs cultivation and watering (see Ps. 107:33–38).

But perhaps a better explanation comes not in spite of the obvious disparity of resources found within the land of ancient Israel, but because of them. Geographically, the land in which the twelve tribes of Israel settled is composed of two fundamentally different ecosystems, defined by a line that marks twelve inches of annual rainfall. Twelve inches of rain, guaranteed every year, is the minimum needed for a farmer to sow

A few goats and a small patch of green pasture in the "land of milk."

The luxurious crown of a date palm in the "land of honey."

and harvest wheat in the area. Barley needs only eight inches, but is a rougher grain, fed mostly to animals and generally considered to be a poor man's wheat substitute. As a dietary staple in biblical Israel, wheat was preferred. Fields need a stable human presence nearby to plow, sow, till, and harvest, to tend and protect. And so in regions on and within the twelve-inch rainfall line, where springs are plentiful, we find permanent settlements throughout the biblical period. Here surplus resources fueled population and economic growth, villages became towns and then cities, and busy traffic fostered open social networks. Of course farmers in ancient Israel planted other things as well, including a variety of orchard crops. We see the conventional list in Deuteronomy 8:7–8:

> *"For the LORD your God is bringing*
> *you into a good land, a land of brooks of*
> *water, of fountains and springs, flowing*
> *forth in valleys and hills; a land of wheat*
> *and barley, of vines and fig trees and*
> *pomegranates, a land of olive oil and*
> *honey."*

Of these, the last named, and sweetest, seems oddly placed, since the list otherwise names plants. Some commentators assume that the honey in this list is the sticky product of the bee, made with the help of the brilliant display of wildflowers that carpets the land every spring. Though bee honey is mentioned in the Bible (in the story of Samson's riddle, for instance; Judg. 14:8), it is more likely that this honey is the syrupy, ultra-sweet paste traditionally made from the fruit of the date palm, a tree otherwise missing from the Deuteronomy 8 list. The Hebrew word *davash* can mean either. Indeed, this is how the Mishnah (*Bikkurim* 1.3) understood the term.

Areas of the land where the rainfall fails to exceed twelve inches annually are much better suited for grazing (Num. 32:1–5). Here we find shepherds living in moveable tents, with herds of sheep and goats. This is a traditional pastoral lifestyle, in which semi-nomads move with the seasons. Because the resources of these areas are thinner, these steppe populations are relatively small in number, and mobile, following available rainfall and always looking for good grazing land. Since eating meat could quickly decimate the flock, the dietary staple for these shepherds is milk and milk-based products, including soft cheeses, yogurts, and derivatives of curdled milk (see Judg. 5:25; Job 10:10).

The twelve-inch line separating these two fundamentally different living areas is relatively easy to see today, demarcated just east and south of the line of villages in Israel and the Palestinian territories where plowed fields give way to open grazing land. It traces the southern end of the hill country of Judah, then bends northward to encompass the wilderness of Judah and much of the Jordan Valley. Of course, we shouldn't think of a firm division in actual practice. Over the millennia, as well as in the biblical text, we can trace an intricate network of social and economic interactions between the settled farmers and seminomadic shepherds, as each developed ways to provide for and protect themselves by entering into social and economic relationships with the other (Gen. 21:22–34; 26:1–33). Only in times of significant crisis, usually brought on by severe drought, did things dissolve into range wars (Judg. 6:1–6).

So now we see that this twelve-inch line marks a land of the shepherd flowing with milk, and a land of the farmer that produces honey. One is a place that, from our Western eyes, looks green, fruitful, productive, noisy, and busy, full of opportunities for a good life; the other a land that is harsh, dry, parched, quiet, empty, and bare. When Moses promised the Israelites that their land would be one flowing with milk and honey, he was standing on the plains of Moab east of Jericho looking square into the barren rise of the wilderness of Judah, devoid of obvious life and yet forming a significant portion of what was to be Israel's longed-for inheritance. After forty years of wilderness grumbling we can imagine their response: "For *this* you hauled us out of Egypt?"

Actually, yes. Egypt was a land of plenty, but it was not where the Israelites belonged.

The line separating permanent settlements from the barren hills of the Judean wilderness is easily seen just beyond the village of Za'atara, a few miles east of Bethlehem. The Dead Sea and rise of the Moab hills are in the distance.

There is good reason to think that Moses, knowing well the human flock God entrusted to him (Ps. 78:52), was quite aware that the land to which he was leading the tribes of Israel was well-suited not just because it was their ancient homeland or because it offered new opportunities for comfort and blessing, but because it represented the realities of human life. The land of milk and the land of honey are both part of the promised land, not in the sense that God promises to give people living there everything they want, but because in both places—in both situations of life—he promises to take care of them—of *us*—no matter what. Neither place is safe; both seek courageous people willing to live under the promises of God.

4. Jerusalem . . .

Signposts:
Jerusalem's
Old City

A trip to Jerusalem is a highlight for visitors to the land of the Bible. Nestled high in the hill country of Judea (and well off the great trunk route that since antiquity has tied Israel to the world beyond), the city has always been a meeting place of east and west, past and present, God and people. There is simply no other place in the world quite like it.

For many, the name Jerusalem evokes images both of the earthly and the eternal. Who isn't captivated by its ancient lure? Who doesn't pause to ponder its future? Throughout the ages, poets, theologians, artists, and writers have sought to portray

Street merchants add to the colorful aura of Jerusalem's Old City.

the essence of this intriguing city. For instance, the Babylonian Talmud, an expansive codification of Jewish oral law dating to the early centuries AD, comments, "Whoever has not seen Jerusalem in its splendor has never seen a lovely city" (*Sukkah* 51b), and "Of the ten measures of beauty that came down to the world, Jerusalem took nine" (*Qiddushin* 49b).

Biblical writers as well held a special fondness for Jerusalem, speaking of it as they would a member of their own family. Indeed, their relationship with Jerusalem was both personal and intense, and infused all aspects of the biblical story, from Genesis to Revelation. The Songs of Ascents (Pss. 120–134), for instance, attest to the sense of loss that the psalmists felt when living away from Jerusalem, and to their unbound joy upon entering its gates:

The wall of the Old City of Jerusalem stretches from Jaffa Gate southward toward modern Mount Zion.

I was glad when they said to me, "Let us go to the house of the LORD." Our feet are standing within your gates, O Jerusalem, Jerusalem, that is built as a city that is compact together; to which the tribes go up, even the tribes of the LORD.

—Psalm 122:1–4

Today, the solid walls of gray-to-golden limestone that encircle the Old City of Jerusalem cradle a fascinating microcosm of life in the Middle East. Everywhere we look, we see things that at first glance seem unfamiliar and exotic. Stepped streets, arched windows, domed roofs, persons in all manner of colorful or dignified dress—these sights and many others add to the aura that Jerusalem is intensely different from back home, wherever that may be.

Visitors from North America are often first struck by the tightness of everything within Jerusalem's walls—building upon building, narrow streets, and a noticeable lack of open space. It's as if everyone in sight wants to lay claim to the same plot of real estate— and, in fact, for the most part, that's exactly the case. For centuries, people lived within the walls of Jerusalem for protection against wild animals, bands of roving bandits, or marching armies. Today, most crowd into the city because they want to be associated with its historic and spiritual roots. It's a difficult place for the claustrophobic—or for those whose prior understandings of the city start to crowd in on them.

Jerusalem, a city whose markets are "compact together."

The psalmist described the layout of Jerusalem well when he noted that it was "built as a city that is compact together" (Ps. 122:3). Like today's Jerusalem, his was a place where life was at the same time both secure and challenging—indeed, both conditions were guaranteed by the city's compactness. It is perhaps apt, then, that for the biblical writers, Jerusalem was a window that revealed what it means for God's people to live in a community with him, a microcosm not just of the Middle East, but of the human soul. Even though biblical Jerusalem may look different from our own hometowns, it sheltered real people facing the same kind of day-to-day struggles that continue to challenge all of God's people. By learning the lessons of Jerusalem's past, we can better face our own struggles today.

5. . . . The Tumultuous City of Peace

While the Old City of Jerusalem may look wildly unfamiliar to an outsider, a closer look at its layout reveals a decidedly Western stamp. The Old City today is roughly square in shape and divided into four quarters of unequal size by two intersecting streets that run at right angles, oriented north-south and east-west. This 90-degree layout is not Middle Eastern at all, but Roman, impressed upon the city in the centuries following the New Testa-

ment after the Roman emperor Hadrian had turned the city into a Greco-Roman *polis* named Aelia Capitolina.

Today, these quarters are informally named after the main groups of people who live there: the Muslim Quarter in the northeastern portion of the city, the Christian Quarter in the northwest, the Armenian Quarter in the southwest, and the Jewish Quarter in the southeast. The Muslim Quarter is the largest in size, while the Jewish Quarter, the smallest, is also the most recently restored. The focal point of each of these quarters is a building or structure held sacred by the

Jerusalem, city of peace.

The tight proximity of Jerusalem's Jewish and Muslim quarters.

majority of its residents: for the Jewish Quarter, it's the Western (or, Wailing) Wall; for the Armenian Quarter, the Church of St. James; for the Christian Quarter, the Church of the Holy Sepulchre; and for the Muslim Quarter, the Haram al-Sharif (Temple Mount).

Altogether about 30,000 people live in the Old City of Jerusalem. They represent a veritable mosaic of religious, ethnic, cultural, social, economic, and nationalistic identities hailing from every region of the Middle East and beyond, all set into an urban frame slightly more than one-half square mile in size. Their everyday interactions on the street and in the marketplace belies deep— and usually suspicious—divisions between the city's many subgroups, most of which are fairly exclusive in their attitudes and behaviors toward others.

Jerusalem has always had a mixed population. This was as true during the time of the Bible as it is today. In the first century AD, Jerusalem was home to persons who identified themselves as Judeans, Galileans, Idumeans, Greeks, and Romans—both Jew and gentile—and during Jewish pilgrimage festivals persons representing every corner of the Mediterranean world packed into the city (see Acts 2:1–11). The Old Testament, too, bears witness to Jerusalem's mixed ethnic base, counting among its residents a variety of peoples including Hittites (2 Sam. 11:3; see also Ezra 9:1–2), Egyptians (1 Kings 9:24), Phoenicians (Neh. 13:16), Ammonites (Neh. 13:7; see also 2:10), and of course the Jebusites, Jerusalem's native population during the time that David conquered the city (2 Sam. 5:6; 24:16).

Family gatherings in the evening shadows along the wall of Jerusalem—a piece of the peace of Jerusalem.

Living in a city packed tight with competing ideologies and jostling with all manner of agendas, it's only appropriate that the writer of Psalm 122 continues:

> *Pray for the peace of Jerusalem: "May they prosper who love you. May peace be within your walls, and prosperity within your palaces." For the sake of my brothers and my friends, I will now say, "May peace be within you." For the sake of the house of the LORD our God, I will seek your good.*
>
> —Psalm 122:6–9

The domes of the Church of the Holy Sepulchre rise above the rooftops of Jerusalem's Christian Quarter.

For the psalmist—as well as all biblical writers—"peace" was not just an absence

of hostilities but the enveloping presence of personal and social well-being that God has intended for his people since the garden of Eden. God's peace is a wholeness that transcends the clamor of ethnicity and culture, binding the vast human mosaic by a frame that only he can put into place. Jerusalem represents both the challenge and the ideal, a world tragically fallen yet gloriously redeemed. The city that is so in need of peace today reminds us of the work that God is doing in our lives, and of our certain future when his work will be complete.

6. Surrounded!

Like people, cities have personalities that are deeper than what can be seen on the surface. Each has, so to speak, a heartbeat and a soul. The biblical writers wanted us to get to know the personality of Jerusalem. As we walk Jerusalem's streets or gaze at it from afar, we, like them, can start to see its "face," the physical characteristics that reflect the life that flows deep within.

And so, it is appropriate that our first look at Jerusalem should touch the contours that make up the face of the city, the hills and valleys that give shape to the places where its residents live. The stone walls and huddled houses of biblical Jerusalem clung to the eastern side of the spiny backbone of the Judean hill country, just off the ridge that divides drainage flowing into the Mediterranean Sea from that descending to the Dead Sea. Steep valleys served as natural defensive lines on all sides but the north. To the east lies the Kidron Valley, which both David and Jesus crossed on their journeys to and from the city (2 Sam. 15:23; Matt. 21:2–11). The Valley of the Son of Hinnom (*gai ben-hinnom*) encircles the ancient city on the west and south (Josh. 18:16); its name likely derived from landed holdings belonging to the Hinnom clan somewhere in its folds. Between, scribing a generally north-south line, is a third valley, not quite as pronounced as these other two but a significant topographical depression nonetheless. The prophet Zephaniah called this wedge through the middle of Jerusalem the "hollow" (*makhtesh*; Zeph. 1:11); the first-century-AD historian Josephus gives us its Roman name, the Tyropoean ("Cheesemakers") Valley. Today, this Central Valley (for such is its mundane modern name) is nearly filled by the rubble of the ages, making it difficult to see; El-Wad Street ("valley" in Arabic), which connects the Western Wall plaza with Damascus Gate, traces its ancient line.

Each of these valleys rises to a higher hill beyond. The Mount of Olives blocks the view of Jerusalemites looking eastward, while the watershed ridge marks the horizon line to the west. The view southward takes in two spurs angling off the watershed ridge; the

The Glick Observation Plaza on Mount Scopus, northeast of the Old City of Jerusalem, is a wonderful spot from which to view the city's strategic hills and valleys.

The City of David, the location of the oldest part of Jerusalem, was a narrow, sloping hill, now covered with houses. The view is from the south, with the Kidron Valley and Mount of Olives on the right.

nearest is home of the Abu Tor neighborhood of Jerusalem, while the furthest is crowned by the stately Government House from the British Mandate, now the headquarters of the United Nations in Jerusalem. To the north, absent a significant natural valley, the hills of old Jerusalem pull gradually upward. The builders of Jerusalem's ancient northern wall compensated for this by digging an artificial moat into the bedrock, part of which is visible today as the rock scarp that forms Skull Hill adjacent to the Garden Tomb.

The topographical shape of ancient Jerusalem, then, was a natural projection, or spur, surrounded by valleys on three sides, beyond which a circle of higher hills rose in all four directions. In this, Jerusalem was certainly not unique. If we visited the sites of the capital cities of all of Judah's hilly neighbors, we would find the situation similar. Samaria, the capital of Israel; Rabbah, the capital of Ammon; Kir (modern Kerak) and Dibon, capitals of Moab; and Bozrah, the capital of Edom, are all similarly situated. We might almost speak of a "geographical genre" that characterizes the topography of the capital cities of these biblical-era kingdoms. But of them, Jerusalem was most pronounced, for it is this Holy City that the rise of the surrounding hills crowds most closely. Indeed, the original location of the biblical city of Jerusalem, the city conquered by David, occupied the lowest end of the narrow spur between the Kidron and Central ("crater") Valleys, making it the lowest inhabited city in the entire spiny central Judean ridge. Standing atop even the highest point of David's Jerusalem, we feel as though we are in the bottom of a bowl (see 2 Kings 21:13), pressed down, its hilly rim rising around us tightly from all directions.

This fact on the ground gave rise to dramatic, and dramatically accurate, language in the biblical Psalms of Ascents, songs that tell us their composers knew the situation of Jerusalem intimately well. First, the hills pose a threat:

*I will lift up my eyes to the mountains; from
where shall my help come? My help comes
from the LORD, who made heaven
and earth.*

—Psalm 121:1–2

Because the city of Jerusalem was often be-
sieged by enemies holding the high ground
that surrounded the city, it is natural that
the writer of Psalm 121 opens his poetic
testimony with a cry of distress: *I'm surrounded! Where does my help come from?*
But he then quickly remembers that the one
who will save him is the maker of heaven
and earth. God not only chose Jerusalem to
be the capital of ancient Judah, he formed
the very shape of the ground on which the
city was built, risk factors and all.

But in another Psalm of Ascents, the psalmist portrays the hills surrounding Jerusalem
quite differently, as a means of safety and
comfort:

*As the mountains surround Jerusalem, so the
LORD surrounds His people from this time
forth and forever.*

—Psalm 125:2

Jerusalem, the Holy City, a place of challenge, redemption, and risk, is a city embraced by its landscape. This, the psalmist
knew, made the geographical setting of his
city a visibly persistent reminder of the reality that God himself embraces his people.
Hugged. Protected. And secure.

7. Living Water

If you had lived in the hill country of Judea during the time of the New Testament, you probably would have preferred to make your home near a spring with a continuous flow of fresh, "living" water. Most of the springs dotting the hillsides of Judea were small, producing little more than a trickle or small brook that was easily lost among the rugged, dry hills of the region. Yet each was adequate for the needs of a family or small group of families who lived in the area, providing clean water for drinking and watering their flocks (Ps. 104:10–11).

If there were no springs in the vicinity, it was possible in places to tap into the underground water table by digging a well—an arduous and unpredictable task, but well

The Jerusalem Temple compound in the time of the New Testament, as depicted in a 1:50 scale model at the Israel Museum, Jerusalem.

The stream at Dan, the strongest source of the Jordan River.

worth the effort if successful. A well could supply unlimited fresh water and often became a common meeting place for villagers or townsfolk. Drawing water from a well was hard work and so typically was done in the cool hours of morning or evening rather than in the heat of the day (Gen. 24:11; 29:7; see also John 4:6–7).

Most Judeans who lived in towns and villages in the time of Jesus, however, drank cistern water. Hewn into bedrock beneath a house, a cistern collected runoff water throughout the rainy season (October through April). If used sparingly, this water kept the family and its livestock alive during the rainless summer months. By the end of the dry season, most cisterns ran low, and a dipped bucket would pick up both water and sludge from the cistern bottom.

Residents of Jerusalem drank cistern water for centuries, right up to the introduction of plumbing in modern times. Nineteenth-century explorers speak of the deplorable living conditions within the walls of Jerusalem, due in large measure to the filth of the streets (see Isa. 10:6; Jer. 38:6) that was washed into the cisterns every rainy season.

A spring of living water flowing into the Wadi Qilt in the Judean wilderness.

Should we assume that living conditions in Jerusalem during the first century AD were any better?

One autumn, Jesus spoke about water when he was in the temple in Jerusalem celebrating the festival of *Sukkot* (Feast of Tabernacles). This eight-day Jewish festival was—and still is—celebrated every year in late September or October. It was during the *Sukkot* festival that the Jews of Jesus' day prayed earnestly for rain—rain to end the drought of the dry season, rain to replenish the fields, and rain to refill the cisterns. It was also at this time of year, in anticipation of the renewed early rain from heaven (see Deut. 11:11, 14), that the people of ancient Judea were most aware of their thirst. And so the gospel of John tells us that:

> *Now on the last day, the great day of the feast, Jesus stood and cried out, saying, "If anyone is thirsty, let him come to Me and drink. He who believes in Me, as the Scripture said, 'From his innermost being will flow rivers of living water.'"*
>
> —John 7:37–38

Drawing water from a cistern is always a good photo-op. The hollowed stone on the left is the watering trough.

Not stale, unsanitary, sludgy cistern water. Not standing, tepid well water. Not even a little brook of fresh spring water. But *rivers* of *living* water, flowing from Jesus and the hearts of those who believe in him. Water that is fully quenching. Water that is healthy. Water that is invigorating. Water that is able to empower us to truly live.

osts:
dern
erusalem

8. Asking "Why?"

Sights of weddings are common in Jerusalem. It's normal to see cars carrying wedding parties, decorated with bright ribbons and flowers; or brides and grooms—though mostly brides—being photographed in picturesque places around the city. The ceremonies for Christian Arabs are usually held in one of Jerusalem's stately stone churches, where the architecture matches the soaring emotions of the young couple. Jewish couples like to be married outside, if the weather is good (that's the case most of the year), enveloped in garden green, on elegant terraces, or within the confines of historic or archaeological sites. It's all very nice, and worth a pause and a picture if you happen by. Then comes the reception, a spare-no-expense occasion that lasts into the wee hours of the morning, with booming music penetrating the nighttime air.

After one particular wedding in Jerusalem a number of years ago, 700 people crowded into Versailles Wedding Hall on the fourth floor of a large building in the Talpiot neighborhood of southeastern Jerusalem to celebrate with the new couple. The music was loud, the mood lively, and the guests began to dance the night away. Suddenly, an hour before midnight that Thursday evening, as the DJ was playing *Lev Zahav*, "Heart of Gold," the floor completely gave way, pitching scores of people downward. The weight of the falling mass collapsed each floor below in turn, opening a huge, gaping crater in the middle of the building. Those left upright stood in shock, waiting endless minutes as the sound of sirens slowly filled the air. The nation, then the world, was gripped by the force of the tragedy.

The next day, Israel's chief rabbi gave a special dispensation to allow the search, rescue, and recovery work to continue through *shabbat*, the Sabbath. By late Saturday afternoon, after everyone who had attended the wedding was accounted for, the search was called off. Altogether twenty-three people died and another 377 were injured in the tragedy, the worst civilian disaster in the history of the modern state of Israel. Almost everybody in Jerusalem, including myself, knew somebody, or knew somebody who knew somebody, who was there. The next day, two powerful car bombs rocked the

Photo shoot of a bride alongside the wall of the Old City of Jerusalem.

center of Jerusalem. It was a pretty rough weekend, and throughout the city people's spirits were shaken.

A memorial garden of twenty-three cypress trees, designed by architect David Guggenheim, honors the memory of the victims of the Versailles Wedding Hall disaster. The gap between the buildings across the street, still hollow two decades after the tragedy, was the site of the hall.

Shortly after the rescue workers began to sift through the site of the disaster, it became apparent that the wedding hall had collapsed because of poor construction and shoddy building materials. It's an all too familiar story, especially in many places outside of North America—a corner cut here, a shekel saved there, and people die in the end.

The rabbi who conducted the wedding ceremony, however, had a different explanation. According to Israeli law, all circumcisions, weddings, and funerals for Jews are to be conducted by Orthodox rabbis, even if the person born, married, or buried is not religious. At times it makes for shocking com-

לזכר

מנחם אסלן   מוטי בועיל   ויקי כהן   שגב ה-שומר   ירוי עקבדיה   משה אתתנול

ברוכם לברכה • שנספו באסון אולמי ורסאי ביום חמישי ביום ג' טיו תשעא

The memorial wall of names. *Lizkor:* "To remember."

mentary. In this case, the rabbi declared that the floor of the hall had fallen because unmarried men and women had been dancing together—"licentiousness punishable by a divine death sentence," he said. After all, he argued, the floor had held during the wedding vows, but collapsed only when the dancing started. Israeli's chief rabbi disagreed; such comments, he said, were contrary to the spirit of Judaism.

What might Jesus have said?

A similar tragedy happened in his day, when the Tower of Siloam, located in the southeastern corner of ancient Jerusalem, also collapsed, killing eighteen people. Public opinion held that the victims must have been terrible sinners who deserved such a fate:

Now on the same occasion there were some present who reported to Him about the Galileans whose blood Pilate had mixed with their sacrifices. And Jesus said to them, "Do you suppose that these Galileans were greater sinners than all other Galileans because they suffered this fate? I tell you, no, but unless you repent, you will all likewise perish. Or do you suppose that those eighteen on whom the tower in Siloam fell and killed them were worse culprits than all the men who live in Jerusalem? I tell you, no, but unless you repent, you will all likewise perish." —Luke 13:1–5

Jesus recognized that sometimes tragedies happen to innocent people. That's the way the world is. Because we live in a fallen world, each of us is prone to fall victim to things that are both tragic and unfair. Like it or not—understand it or not—it's part of life. At the same time, Jesus used the tragedies of his day to point to a larger truth, namely, that all persons stand in need of repentance and restoration before God.

What we receive and what we endure are both due to the sovereignty, and the grace, of God. That's reality, but it's also the gospel.

9. Eternal Hope

Signposts:
Tekoa Wadi;
Haritun Cave

Baseball is a harbinger of spring in America, the season when hope springs eternal and even the cellar dwellers still have a shot at the World Series. Baseball is becoming one of the markers of spring in Israel as well. When he was twelve, my son Ben played on the Jerusalem Cadets, one of the youth baseball teams in Israel. While the level of play is not up to that of teams in the Americas, the experience was wholesome for the kids, coaches, and parents alike.

That year, on the first Friday in May, the Cadets played against a team from Efrat, an Israeli settlement town in the West Bank between Bethlehem and Hebron. Because Israeli-Palestinian tensions were running particularly high, the Efrat team traveled to

The Tekoa (Haritun) Wadi, southeast of Bethlehem.

The two square openings in the lower left are doorways of the Byzantine cave-house in which the bodies of the two boys, Kobi and Yosef, were found.

Jerusalem in an armored bus, with—as is common even in times of relative peace—an armed guard. The guard, who doubled as the Efrat coach, left his machine gun, without the clip, in the dugout with a pile of baseball equipment. I asked him how it would work as a bat, and he wasn't amused. One of the Efrat players wore a Yankees cap as he took his position on the field. Ah, Americana! The game was competitive yet friendly, and the Cadets won, their first victory in three attempts so far that young season.

The following Wednesday, the pitcher of my son's team, a boy named Aaron, was watching an international news station on cable television. The network was covering a story of two boys from Tekoa (a town neighboring

Efrat), ages thirteen and fourteen, whose bodies had just been found in the ruins of a Byzantine monk's house built into a small cave on the southern slope of Nahal Tekoa (the Haritun Wadi), a dry, steep-edged canyon not far from their homes. They had been murdered while skipping school to go hiking in the wadi, their heads smashed by large rocks. A group called Hezbollah-Palestine claimed responsibility for the attack. Aaron immediately recognized one of the boys as Kobi, a member of the Efrat team that the Cadets had faced on the ball diamond just five days before. Two days later, the *Jerusalem Post* newspaper carried a large picture of Kobi taken on a recent trip to New York. He wore a big smile and a Yankees cap.

How do we respond to something like this?

The prophet Jeremiah gives us a clue. Jeremiah lived in Jerusalem when the entire city was destroyed by the Babylonians. Thousands of innocent people were killed, some no doubt smashed to pieces by rocks, if the cry of revenge found in Psalm 137:8–9 is any indication. The book of Lamentations captures Jeremiah's intense shock and grief in witnessing this tragedy of untold proportions:

> *How lonely sits the city that was full of people! She has become like a widow who was once great among the nations! She who was a princess among the provinces has become a forced laborer! She weeps bitterly in the night and her tears are on her cheeks; she has none to comfort her. . . . "O wall of the daughter of Zion, let your*

tears run down like a river day and night;
give yourself no relief, let your eyes have no
rest. "—Lamentations 1:1–2; 2:18

Jeremiah's cries are as real today as they were in his day, but so is his resolve to survive. This was a man of faith, and in the middle of his overwhelming darkness he saw a single, bright beam of light:

This I recall to my mind, therefore I have hope. The LORD's lovingkindnesses indeed never cease, for His compassions never fail. They are new every morning; great is Your faithfulness. "The LORD is my portion," says my soul, "Therefore I have hope in Him."

—Lamentations 3:21–24

Jeremiah had no intention of ignoring the tragedy of his day, or of retreating into a philosophy of life that offered only safe answers. He knew that God was faithful—the brutal facts of life don't change that—and continued to wait on his mercies. Every day, Jeremiah knew, came with new opportunities for God to be gracious to his people. For Jeremiah, even in tragedy, the hope that is grounded in the confidence of God sprang eternal.

10. It's Christmas! (Maybe)

Christmas is a wonderful time of the year. Family get-togethers, candlelight services, decorated trees with brightly wrapped gifts, crackling fireplaces, and deep snow— these are some of the images of Christmas that fill our hearts. The classic Currier and Ives depictions of Christmas that became popular over 100 years ago have helped give shape to a holiday experience that is most typical of New England or the upper Midwest, yet somehow remains proper even for people living in Miami or San Diego. Even our favorite Christmas hymns prompt us to picture that first Christmas in Bethlehem as something typical of late December

A Christmastime evening in Manger Square, Bethlehem.

in America's snow belt, speaking of "a cold winter's night that was so deep" and "the bleak midwinter" where "snow had fallen, snow on snow."

When was Jesus born? Almost certainly not on December 25th: that date was apparently adopted by Christians in the fourth century AD as a concession to pagan midwinter Roman festivals. But if not December 25th, then when?

Two clues in Luke's account of Jesus' birth suggest that Jesus was probably born in mid- to late summer or early autumn. Both are found in Luke 2:8:

Shepherds and their flocks frequent fields after the grain is harvested in early summer.

> *In the same region there were some shepherds staying out in the fields . . .*

The first clue is that the shepherds who hurried to Bethlehem that first Christmas night were watching their flocks "out in the fields." Is this where shepherds would be expected to be in the wintertime? Certainly not! The growing season for grain in Judea has always begun in November, when farmers plow their fields in anticipation of the winter rains. The fields around Bethlehem are typically planted with wheat and barley (see Ruth 1:22; 2:23); barley is harvested in late spring, and wheat after the rains stop in early summer. While wintertime fields filled with tender shoots of grain would make great dining for flocks of sheep and goats, from the point of view of the farmer who planted the field a hungry horde such as this would be most unwelcome guests! Rather, during the winter rainy season shepherds drive their flocks onto the uncultivated hillsides or

The entrance to the grotto under the altar of the Church of the Nativity in Bethlehem, which encloses a cave where an ancient tradition holds that Jesus was born.

59

These houses at Shawbak, in the highlands of Edom, are typical of those built into the rocky hills of the land of ancient Israel for millennia. Their back rooms are natural caves which could serve as living spaces for people or animals.

out to the edges of the wilderness of Judah east of Bethlehem where they can graze on the thin covering of grass that sprouts by midwinter.

Yet summertime is a different matter altogether. As the rains of winter give way to the cloudless skies of summer, the farmers harvest their fields, leaving the stubble behind. It is specifically during the hot summer months that the fallow fields of Bethlehem provide excellent grazing land for a shepherd's hungry flocks—and that with the blessing of the local farmers, who appreciate the ability of the sheep and goats to fertilize their fields.

. . . keeping watch over their flock by night.

Because Bethlehem lies at an elevation of 2,300 feet above sea level, winter nights can be miserably cold and wet. This is surely the time of year that any flocks that might be in the vicinity of Bethlehem would have to be sheltered at night, either in a cave or a manmade enclosure. Yet Luke's account of Jesus' birth implies that when the shepherds tended their sheep at night, they were out in the open, beneath a starry sky. Bethlehem shepherds may well camp in the open throughout the endlessly warm nights of summer, but never at night in midwinter. It's just too cold.

One year back in the late Byzantine period when I was in high school, the pastor of our church decided to celebrate Christmas in July, with the tree and all the trimmings. His idea was that we would collect gifts for the overseas missionary families that the church supported, then mail them in time to be received by December 25th. In those days international mail was pretty unreliable. I don't recall him mentioning that Jesus' birth may actually have been closer to July 25th than December 25th, but no matter—it was a great idea. Christmas is always a wonderful time of the year, even if it celebrates an event that might have happened in the summer.

11. The Rival King

The cone-shaped hill of Herodium dominates the Judean skyline southeast of Bethlehem. It is one of several mountain fortresses built by Herod the Great in the wilderness east, southeast, and northeast of Jerusalem toward the close of the first century BC in order to protect Rome's desert frontier and strengthen his own iron grip on the country. In addition to Herodium, Herod fortified Hyrcania in a chalky plain in the wilderness of Judah, Masada on the Dead Sea's barren western shore, Machaerus overlooking the Dead Sea from the east,

Cypros above Jericho, and Alexandrium towering over the central Jordan Valley. It was in these fortresses, all of which were outfitted with elegant palaces, that Herod basked in the opulence of Rome far from the public eye—or imprisoned his political opponents. Each fortress also provided a safe haven should conditions in Jerusalem become too volatile for the despot king.

The hill into which Herodium was built sits on a geological seam that separates the rolling limestone terrain and arable soil around Bethlehem from the utterly barren, chalky hills of the wilderness of Judah. The view from the top is magnificent and

Herodium (right), and the hill that Herod's workmen lowered, in part to remove anything in the vicinity that might overshadow their king's eventual burial place.

Visitors walk among the remains of Herod's pleasure palace inside Herodium.

encompasses the sweep of the southern expanse of Herod's kingdom.

A sharp eye will notice that the hill adjacent to Herodium is also flat-topped but much lower than the fortress; apparently Herod's workmen sheared its top in order to provide building materials for Herodium, creating a lofty visual effect at the same time. Inside Herodium Herod built a banqueting hall, a bath complex, and a colonnaded garden, all in the latest Roman style. At Herodium's outer base he installed a huge water pool with an island gazebo; the first-century Jewish historian Josephus called it Herod's "pleasure grounds" (*Ant.* 15.324). The water for both bath and pool was carried to Herodium by an aqueduct that channeled water from springs at Artas, south of Bethlehem. Herod was, after all, king, and enjoyed every royal prerogative he could muster.

The paranoia that prompted Herod to build these fortresses was well founded. He had already fled Jerusalem once, at the beginning of his reign, barely escaping with his life. When Herod first became Rome's puppet ruler over Judea in 40 BC, he faced intense political upheaval from Jewish nationalists who were bent on restoring the independent state that had been taken from them by Rome two decades before. At the same time, Judea was also invaded by the Parthians, rulers of a mighty empire in Persia and Mesopotamia. Many Jews welcomed this Parthian invasion, sensing in it an opportunity to overthrow Herod and the Roman yoke. Facing a combined assault, Herod fled, passing the very hill that he would later fortify as Herodium. Eventually making his way to Rome, he received the blessing and

A reconstructed scale model of the monument that Herod built to mark the location of his tomb on the northern face of Herodium—and to memorialize in stone something of his outsized ego. The original was visible from Jerusalem.

support of Caesar, then returned to literally slash and burn his way to a kingdom.

In the end, Herod got what he deserved. Dying an excruciating death, he was buried at Herodium amid pomp, splendor, and great public relief. Just before he died, however, Herod's paranoia ran wild. He killed his own heir-apparent sons, thinking they were plotting against him. And then, of all things, men from the east appeared in Jerusalem, looking for the true king of the Jews:

> *"Where is He who has been born King of the Jews? For we saw His star in the east and have come to worship Him."*
>
> —Matthew 2:2

Throughout his entire reign, Herod had prepared for, and feared, an event like this. What must he have thought? "The Parthians have returned! They want to install the legitimate king!" His response was brutal (Matt. 2:16–18) but true to form.

In the pervasive shadow of Herodium lay the little town of Bethlehem. It was there that God again stepped into human history, quietly and without human pretense, just when Herod spun out of control. And the kingdom that he established through the manger of Bethlehem, so very different from Herod's, continues to meet the "hopes and fears of all the years" even today.

12. The Journey Home

The magi are among the most interesting and mysterious people to travel across the pages of Scripture. They were, in our vocabulary, more astronomers than astrologers, probing the nighttime skies with mathematical exactness and a deep-seated belief that somehow, the movement of the stars was connected to events on earth. Perhaps the magi were urban scholars, at home among the academies and libraries of Babylon, fastidiously preserving the remnants of a 4,000-year-old Mesopotamian civilization. Yet they also knew the stories and prophecies of the Jews who had been residents of Babylonia since the exile almost 600 years before (Gen. 49:10; Num. 24:17; Isa. 60:3).

The Visit of the Magi, depicted in stained glass in the Church of St. Catherine, Bethlehem.

The Nabateans who controlled the spice route from Yemen to Gaza left marks of their activities on rock faces along the way. These are in Wadi Rum, Jordan. It was this route that provided the frankincense and myrrh that the magi presented to the Christ child.

And so the magi set off on a most remarkable journey to find a baby who was beginning an even more remarkable journey of his own. They would have followed one of the great caravan routes of antiquity, north, west, and then south along the bend of the Fertile Crescent toward Judea. By doing so, they traveled roughly the same path that Abraham had trod two millennia before as he left first his home, then his family, for a land known only to God (see Gen. 11:31–12:5). And for these urban magi, like the seminomad Abraham, this was not only the journey of a lifetime, but a matter of tremendous personal risk, taking them far from their comfort zone and into the great unknown.

Geographical logic suggests that once the magi reached Damascus, they probably would have continued to follow the caravan route due south, toward the Arabian Peninsula. It was this ancient highway that supplied the Roman world with exotic goods such as frankincense and myrrh—aromatic gum resins—and even gold. By the time of the birth of Jesus, the Arabia-to-Damascus spice route was controlled by the Nabateans, known today as the builders of the rose-red city of Petra. Perhaps it was somewhere along this route that the magi purchased their gifts for the Christ child (see Isa. 60:4–7).

Geographical logic also suggests that the magi left the caravan route at a point northeast of the Dead Sea and turned toward Jerusalem, crossing through Jericho on the way. If so, they would have passed by the shadow of the large and over-the-top winter palace of King Herod, which he built to bring the wealth and comfort of Rome to a most inhospitable land. Today, just enough of Herod's Jericho palace remains to indicate the personal grandeur he sought to display to his subjects: "You're in *my* land now," it said. "Don't cross me." Did the magi suspect what a meeting with this despot might bring?

They pressed on. Climbing through the rugged wilderness of Judah, the magi reached Jerusalem and eventually Herod himself. They were far from home, vulnerable, alone, and without access to networks of resource and aid—yet face-to-face with one of the most ruthless and clever rulers the world has ever known. Undaunted, they continued to Bethlehem:

When they saw the star, they rejoiced exceedingly with great joy. After coming into the house they saw the Child with Mary His mother; and they fell to the ground and worshiped Him.

—Matthew 2:10–11

Irrespective of their origin and route of travel, the magi almost certainly arrived in Bethlehem by camel. And what would a modern manger scene be without them?

Facing insurmountable difficulties, the magi were resolute in their goal. The passage of time, personal hardships, and dangers both expected and unknown all failed to

sway their advance. Overcoming every obstacle, the travelers persisted—and rejoiced when at last they gazed at the divine Child face-to-face.

Eventually, we read, the magi returned to their own country (Matt. 2:12). They were no more at home in the land of promise than Abraham had been (see Heb. 11:8–16). Yet at the same time, both glimpsed the face of God by journeying into his land.

Where is your journey taking you? Eventually we're heading home, to live forever with Jesus. But in the meantime, while our journeys may be hard, we, too, have opportunities to commune with God. And whenever we do, it's as if we're already there.

13. Lifted Up

Grape vines are one of the seven species of fruitful plants that best characterize the land of Israel (Deut. 8:7–8). Luxurious, with sweet, juicy fruit that can be eaten whole or made into wine, the vine became, for ancient Israel, one of the most vibrant symbols of a blessed life. Biblical writers were fond of comparing the nation of Israel to a flourishing vine, one whose goodness filled the hills:

> *You removed a vine from Egypt. . . . You cleared the ground before it, and it took deep root and filled the land.*
>
> —Psalm 80:8–9

> *My well-beloved had a vineyard on a fertile hill. He dug it all around, removed its stones, and planted it with the choicest vine. . . . For the vineyard of the* LORD *of hosts is the house of Israel, and the men of Judah His delightful plant.*
>
> —Isaiah 5:1–2, 7

Indeed, the adage "Judah and Israel lived in safety, every man under his vine and his fig tree" (1 Kings 4:25) became the template for the good life for an ancient Israelite living under the care and protection of the favor of God (Mic. 4:4; Zech. 3:10).

Some of our favorite images of healthy, productive vineyards come from places like Napa Valley, California, or the Loire Valley in France. Here, well-trimmed vines dress long rows of straight-lined trellises, hanging heavy with large clusters of plump, juicy grapes. Israelis are very proud of their vineyards as well, which stretch in trellised rows across hills from the Negev to the Golan Heights and produce vintage that can compete with some of the best wines in the world.

In his practical treatise *On Agriculture*, written in the late first century BC, the Latin statesman Varro compared methods of growing vines across the Roman world. He discussed the different kinds of trellises found in vineyards throughout the western and central Mediterranean, but reported that in the eastern part of the Roman Empire, which would have included the land of ancient Israel, vines were grown without

A spreading vine in the Judean hills southeast of Hebron, lifted up on an old tire so that the grapes can hang freely.

trellises. How so? According to Varro, vine growers in the eastern Mediterranean allowed the main branches of their vines to run along the ground, lifting them on forked sticks only when the grapes first appeared.

Springtime in the Judean hills, as grape leaves first appear. A budding fig tree stands in the background.

After the harvest, the branches were lowered to the ground to hibernate until the next growing season (Varro, *On Agriculture*, 1.8.1–7). This method of tending a vineyard, tried and true, appears in the one of Ezekiel's parables:

> *"Then [the vine] sprouted and became*
> *a low, spreading vine with its branches*
> *turned toward [the messenger of God], but*
> *its roots remained under it."*

—Ezekiel 17:6

The practice persists among the Arab farmers in parts of the West Bank to this day, though they typically use large, flat stones or even old tires rather than forked sticks to raise the budding branches.

It seems that Jesus was familiar with this method of tending vines. Drawing from a rich heritage that likened Israel to the vine, he told his disciples, who were seated around the Passover table just hours before his arrest, that he was the true vine and his Father, God himself, the vinedresser. Then he gave a tutorial in tending vines, with his disciples, each a branch "in him," the object of the lesson. Jesus proceeded in proper vine tending sequence:

> *"Every branch in Me that does not bear fruit, He takes away; and every branch that bears fruit, He prunes it so that it may bear more fruit. . . . If anyone does not abide in Me, he is thrown away as a branch and dries up; and they gather them, and cast them into the fire and they are burned."*
>
> —John 15:2, 6

We usually read the verb "takes away" negatively, as a dire warning, but our first-century expert in east Mediterranean viticulture prompts us to think otherwise. In his treatise, Varro stated that "the only branches that are raised from the ground are those which give promise of producing fruit" (*On Agriculture*, 1.8.6). In other words, the branches that abide in the vine and are not yet fruit-bearing (but show every evidence of being so) are "taken away"; that is, taken away from the ground on which they lie dormant so that they can produce fruit. A better English translation, now that we see the actual practice of vine tending in Jesus' Judea, is that they are "lifted up." Then, as the branches and young tendrils start to produce grapes, the vines are pruned here and there so that their fruit can develop further. It is only the branches that are wholly unproductive (either because they are not well connected to the main trunk of the vine and draw no sustenance from it or are suckers without nodes to produce fruit), that are removed, though they are still useful as fuel for the fire.

Jesus was not unaware of the details of the normal lives of everyday folk. He knew how to build buildings, how to sow seed, how to catch fish, and how to care for vineyards. And he used the things that were wholly part of everyday life to help his followers better understand who he was. Not bearing fruit yet? I will lift you up so you can. Already bearing fruit? It may hurt a bit, but let me help you bear more. Don't want to bear fruit? In God's economy you may still be useful to others, though not to your own benefit nor in the manner of your own design. That's provident grace. But it's far better to abide in him.

14. Grief Embraced

Signposts: Jerusalem, Mount of Olives, Garden of Gethsemane

For centuries, the lower, western slopes of the Mount of Olives have been prime Jerusalem real estate for the living, but also for the dead. From at least biblical times, areas of the mount that are at eye level for Jerusalemites gazing eastward across the Kidron Valley have held tombs of the dearly departed, a persistent reminder of what it means to belong to a very special place. Old photos show that up until modern times, before the urban growth of Jerusalem so quickly swallowed up nearly every open space on the mountain, wide swaths of cultivatable land filled plots of ground between these ancient cemeteries. Indeed, the depth and quality of soil on the western, lower part of the Mount of Olives is quite good, thanks to eons of winter rains that have washed soils down from the slopes above. As a result, the lowest part of the Mount of Olives has always been dotted with orchards, especially olive orchards, hence the mountain's name. We can rightly imagine clusters of olive trees forming rich bands of green, a color of life; interspersed by

Olive trees in Kidron Valley. "Absalom's Pillar," which is actually a tomb marker from the time of the New Testament, stands behind, with the Silwan Village in the distance.

tombs, reminders of death, framing the eastern horizon of Jesus' Jerusalem.

A gnarled olive tree within the enclosed garden of the Church of All Nations, the most frequently visited site marking the Garden of Gethsemane.

The biblical Hebrew term *gan* indicates a protected area under cultivation, a plot of ground typically embraced by a stone wall where an ancient landowner and his family, likely for generations, enjoyed toil and its rewards. The best English translation of *gan* is "garden," a place of quiet provision. Jesus often met with his disciples in such a garden on the western slope of the Mount of Olives, within the fold of the Kidron Valley (John 18:1–2). Its owner, by implication, seems to have been one of his followers. This particular garden had a name: Gethsemane (Matt. 26:36; Mark 14:32).

Christian tradition marks two spots as possible locations of the garden of Gethsemane. One, the grounds of the Church of Mary Magdalene, preserves Russian Orthodox memory. Graced by soaring onion domes recently plated by 24-karat gold, the church was built by Czar Alexander III in 1888. The site is open to the public only occasionally during the week. If the gate is open, a passerby would do well to stop in to visit the spacious, well-kept grounds and the interior of the ornate church.

A second possible location of the garden of Gethsemane is at the Church of All Nations, a site under the custody of the Franciscans. The present church was erected in 1924 over remains of one dating from the fourth century AD built to commemorate Jesus' visit to the garden. The building encloses the Rock of Agony, on which Jesus is remembered to have sweat "like drops of blood" as he prayed (Luke 22:44). The windows are sheets of purple alabaster, darkly translucent so that even under the bright sun it is always midnight under a full moon inside. Within the compound and adjacent to the church are olive trees whose age should be counted in centuries, not millennia. The first-century-AD historian Josephus mentions that Jerusalem and its outlying regions were stripped of timber to support the Roman siege in AD 70 (*Jewish War* 5.264). The trees of Gethsemane must have been felled in the process. Still, popular tradition holds that the trees growing in the garden today are the same ones under which Jesus knelt; stately and sedate, they don't mind the compliment.

It was a moment of high melodrama, probably close to midnight, given the normal length of a Passover meal. The moon was full, high in the sky, with a springtime chill and, likely, wind rustling the darkened olive leaves that cast wild shadows under the moonlight. Tombs lay nearby, beckoning; night sounds filled the air outside the ancient city's walls. Jesus had a choice: stay and face the cross, or scramble up and over the crest of the mountain out of reach of everyone who might want to do him in, then slip back to the quiet certainty of Galilee. His closest followers were asleep—they would never have to know the details.

"Yet not my will, but Yours be done."

—Luke 22:42

Gethsemane. The name comes from *gat shemen*, Hebrew for "oil press." Tour guides and homiliticians speak of the name representing the sweat squeezed from Jesus' brow, like oil from a press, a combination of dread, grief, and resolve under intense pressure. He was betrayed when most vulnerable.

Every summer I teach a short course on the life and times of Jesus. For two weeks we follow Jesus' journeys from Bethlehem to Nazareth and Capernaum with lots of places in between, then finally, like him, resolutely set our faces to Jerusalem (see Luke 9:51). We stop at the garden of Gethsemane on the next to last day of the trip. Nearly everyone taking the course is engaged in the material, focused and eager to discover. The last day is always a free day in Jerusalem. Most spend it shopping among the lively markets of the Old City. On one particular last day a few years ago, one of my students, a woman in her early thirties, chose instead to return to the garden, her inner being heavy with intention. She brought a friend to share her soul. A couple of years before, her husband had left her for someone else, without warning. She was stunned. Angry. Adrift. Unsure of the future. Hoping against hope that life could go back to how it once had been. And now her journey of recovery had brought her to the garden where her Lord had faced agony and betrayal even she couldn't imagine. She took her wedding band, once a circle of unending love, now a

The façade of the Church of All Nations, with the golden onion domes of the Russian Church of Mary Magdalene, an alternative site for the Garden of Gethsemane, above.

hollow symbol of love betrayed, and threw it among the gnarled olive trees where it was embraced by the soft soil of this once blood-sweat ground. After a hard-fought journey with her Savior, this was the only place it belonged.

"My soul is deeply grieved . . . remain here and keep watch with Me."

—Matthew 26:38

She did. And became whole.

15. Sanctified Memories

Memories. Things that remind us of where we've been, who we are, and what we've done. Usually memories are things we cherish; sometimes they're things we hope to forget. In the portion of his autobiography that recounted his conversion to Christianity, St. Augustine of Hippo (AD 354–430) mused about the nature of memory as a way of knowing who God is. In the process, he remarked: "great is the power of memory, exceedingly great,—an inner chamber large and boundless!" but then asked, "Where in my memory do You abide, O Lord? What manner of chamber have You formed for Yourself?" (*Confessions* 10.8.15, 25). We can easily expand Augustine's introspective

A portion of the cliff adjacent to the Garden Tomb resembles the face of a skull.

The Garden Tomb, infused with quiet expectancy.

inquiry about the power of memory to the efforts of the early church, which sought to know God, at least in part, by remembering specific events in the life of Jesus at specific places where they were thought to have occurred. In doing so, the actions of Jesus not only were authenticated for them in time and place but became signposts for generations of believers to follow. The Roman province of Syria Palaestina became *Terra Sancta*, the Holy Land, a place worthy of pilgrimage, in the process.

Of course not everything that Jesus did has been recorded for memory (see John 21:25). But of the many things that are, none is more important for the life of the church than his death and resurrection outside Jerusalem.

*Then they brought Him to the
place Golgotha, which is translated,
Place of a Skull.*

—Mark 15:22

Golgotha is the Aramaic word for "skull." The Latin form is *calvaria*, Calvary. It's an evocative name if there ever was one. Perhaps this place of crucifixion got its name because there were skulls there. Or perhaps the shape of the place, or that of a nearby cliff, came to resemble a skull (there was ancient quarrying in the area). Or, the name may have stuck to the place simply because it evoked the absence of life.

Two places in Jerusalem hold the memory of the event. The primary site is the Church of the Holy Sepulchre, consecrated on September 13, AD 335, over a place that Helena, mother of the Roman emperor Constantine I, identified as the location of Jesus' crucifixion, burial, and resurrection. According to early church memory, she found a piece of Jesus' cross in a cave there. We can probably assume that local Christians, who already had venerated the place from at least the late first century AD, were content enough to let the mother of the emperor take credit for "discovering" the location. In any case, nothing disqualifies the site from being authentic: it was outside the wall of Jerusalem in Jesus' day, on a major road leading into the city, in the area of a garden, and with tombs dating to the first century nearby. All of this has been shown from archaeology and geography. The collective weight of Christian memory, which is a pretty powerful force, has settled here nicely for nearly 2,000 years. The current structure, with a dark, windowless, and ornately Orthodox interior of incense and stone, includes portions of walls from as early as the Byzantine period and houses chapels that mark elements of the story. Although anyone can visit the Church of the Holy Sepulchre—and hundreds of thousands of pilgrims do every year—rights to hold services are limited to five Eastern Orthodox churches—the Greeks, Armenians, Copts, Syrians, and Ethiopians—and the Roman Catholics represented by the Franciscans. The Orthodox groups prefer to call the building the Church of the Resurrection, a name that resonates with many Protestant visitors as well.

A short walk through Damascus Gate and north of the current wall of the Old City of Jerusalem brings visitors to the beautiful grounds of the Garden Tomb. This is an outdoor site with simple ornamentation, maintained in the style of a tranquil English garden. A quarried cliff face once resembling a skull is visible to the east. The tomb is one of several in the area dating to the Iron Age (the eighth to sixth centuries BC); the others are on the grounds of the Saint-Étienne Monastery belonging to the French Dominican order, behind the stone wall that frames the tomb. In this place of active worship and quiet reflection the staff of the Garden Tomb ensures that no visitor leaves without encountering the reality of the death, burial, and resurrection of Jesus.

How might the eyewitnesses have remembered Jesus' crucifixion? Most probably didn't. "Those passing by" (Matt. 27:39), some anonymous bystanders (Matt. 27:47–48) and some unnamed officials, both Roman and Jewish (Matt. 27:41), had no particular reason to keep long memories of the event. Others, whose names we do know, watched "from a distance" (Mark 15:40); why so, we can only imagine, though horror and denial likely played a role. These included Mary the mother of James and Joseph, and Salome. Only John gives the names of eyewitnesses who stood next to the cross: Jesus' mother, her sister, Mary the wife of

A procession of Greek Orthodox priests enters the Church of the Holy Sepulchure.

Clopas, Mary Magdalene, and "the disciple whom He loved," likely John himself (John 19:25–27). Their memories were the most acute, seared by the stench of blood, the contorted body shape, the raspy last gasp of life. None of the Gospels mention where Matthew, Mark, or Luke might have been.

The altar of the crucifixion in the Church of the Holy Sepulchre, marking the place most sacred to Christian memory.

Their memories must have been shaped in large part by the testimony of the eyewitnesses (Luke 1:2). And where was Peter? All we know is that he was an eyewitness the morning after the morning after, to the just opened, forever empty tomb (John 20:1–10).

Our own memories of an event—of any event—may vary. Likely they are shaped in part by the collective memories of others who witnessed the same things. That "inner chamber large and boundless" may hold a fairly accurate picture of whatever it is that happened, or, selective as our memories tend to be, it may be well off the mark. Whatever form they take, our memories are crucial for the role they play in keeping our connection to people and things that preceded us alive.

But they don't change what actually happened.

Our faith is grounded in the reality of the resurrection. Is our memory of the resurrection of Jesus better represented by the Holy Sepulchre? By the name Church of the Resurrection? By the Garden Tomb? Or by something or somewhere else? *How* the resurrection is remembered is far less important than *that* it happened. And in allowing others to hold on to their memories of that event, we affirm its certainty for us as well.

16. A Most Unexpected Encounter

As might be expected with a careful historian such as Luke, his is the only gospel that gives specific geographical information about a post-resurrection appearance of Jesus.

And behold, two of them were going that very day to a village named Emmaus, which was about seven miles from Jerusalem. —Luke 24:13

Here we have two place names, one a very well-known city, the other a village, with a road connecting them (Luke 24:32, 35) and the specific distance between, mentioned by Luke in *stadia* but converted in virtually all English Bibles into miles. We are also told what day it was (the same day as Jesus' resurrection) and something about the time of day: they approached Emmaus as it was "getting toward evening" (Luke 24:29). If we make the logical assumption that the two travelers (one whom we learn is named Cleopas; the other remains forever anonymous; Luke 24:18) were taking the customary route from Jerusalem to Emmaus, it ought to be fairly simple for us to locate the event in time and place, and even to recreate the walk today.

But we can't move so fast. When it comes to giving the distance between Jerusalem and Emmaus, we find differences in the early Greek manuscripts of Luke. Some read "one

hundred sixty stadia," a bit under nineteen miles, while others give the distance as "sixty stadia," or seven miles. To complicate matters further, we are not sure if the distance given is one-way or round trip, the latter perhaps a more practical way to measure local travel in the ancient world. So church tradition and modern historical inquiry have settled on four options for the location of Emmaus. The one that has received the most attention is an Emmaus mentioned by Josephus (*Jewish War* 2.60–65, 71; 4.444) out where the hill country of Judah meets the foothills, just under nineteen miles west of Jerusalem. The site is remembered today by the Arabic name 'Imwas, which preserves

Curbstones from the Roman road connecting Jerusalem with Emmaus, dating to the century after the events of the gospels.

the name. By the fourth century AD this city was a thriving urban center and had taken on a Greek name, Nicopolis. Eusebius, bishop of Caesarea at the time, identified Nicopolis as the site of Emmaus in his *Onomasticon* (456), and all of Byzantine memory fell in line. Today, remains of a large Byzantine church from the fifth and sixth centuries AD mark the spot.

The Bibles used by the crusaders in the twelfth century read that Emmaus was sixty stadia from Jerusalem, and so the Knights Hospitaller located Emmaus at Qaryet el-Enab, modern Abu Ghosh, adjacent to a comfortable caravanserai (a traveler's way-station) only seven miles west of Jerusalem. The crusader church that they built to commemorate Jesus' visit remains the largest building in the core of the oldest part of Abu Ghosh today. After the crusaders were driven from the Holy Land, the main road to Jerusalem moved somewhat north, through Nabi Samwil. With it, the medieval memory of Emmaus shifted to the small village of el-Qubeibeh west of Nabi Samwil, which was also, conveniently, about sixty stadia, or seven miles, from Jerusalem.

The fourth site is another Emmaus that Josephus said lay only thirty furlongs (thirty-two stadia) west of Jerusalem (*Jewish War* 7.217), a place corresponding with the modern Israeli town of Motza. Motza also preserves the name Emmaus, though in Hebrew. The remains of the ancient village are in the bottom of the steep Sorek Valley about three and a half miles west of the Old City of

Jerusalem, which would have made the total journey about sixty stadia round trip.

The Emmaus remembered at 'Imwas, the Emmaus remembered at Abu Ghosh, and the Emmaus remembered at Motza are all located on the same natural route, a road that was paved by the Romans in the second century AD to connect Jerusalem with the port of Joppa. The route more or less parallels modern Israeli Highway 1 today. Of the three, Motza best fits the timeline of Luke 24, in which the disciples walked to the village at conversation-pace, arrived "toward evening" (in mid- to late afternoon), and were able to hurry back to Jerusalem to catch the disciples still awake that night.

Cleopas and his traveling companion were perplexed and distraught as they made their

The valley that once carried the Roman road from Jerusalem to Emmaus is badly in need of restoration today.

way to Emmaus that resurrection day afternoon, deep in conversation about what had happened in Jerusalem the last few days. Jesus pulled up beside them, listening. "Their eyes were prevented from recognizing Him," we read (Luke 24:16). Then he spoke, first by asking questions, as rabbis who want to draw their disciples into conversation typically do. It was only after hearing the agony of their hearts that Jesus allowed them into his.

Beginning with Moses and with all the prophets, He explained to them the things concerning Himself in all the Scriptures.

—Luke 24:27

I wish one of them had had a recording device. Instead, it was left to the writers of the New Testament and millennia of theologians since to work out the details.

That evening, Jesus ate his first supper after the Last one. Recognizing him only as he broke and blessed the bread, Cleopas and his companion hurried back to Jerusalem, their hearts stirred as they walked into the light of a nearly full, post-Passover moon rising over the Holy City.

"Were not our hearts burning within us while He was speaking to us on the road . . . ?"

—Luke 24:32

The route these disciples must have taken from Emmaus (Motza) to Jerusalem is known, with a portion surveyed and mapped by archaeologists. Yet today it's a mess, and nearly impassable. The portion from Motza to the western outskirts of modern Jerusalem follows the bottom of a narrow, rising gorge. Laid along its length, above ground, is a massive pipeline that carries fresh water to Jerusalem. Electrical pylons also march up the gorge, their heavy concrete bases sunk into the ground. Much of the way is covered by heaps of stone and rubble, some from natural erosion, most as construction debris; a tangled mass of undergrowth obscures the rest. It takes tremendous effort to follow the Emmaus road today; perhaps it did for these two disciples as well.

For us, on our own walk with Jesus, that Emmaus Road junk could be anything: stuff put there by others; stuff that's there through faults of our own; stuff we just find in the way. Whatever the source, it's stuff that keeps us from seeing, from understanding, and from walking how and where we should. And when Jesus does appear, we often don't recognize him.

Until we do. And that's the beginning of grace. Like with Cleopas and his companion, that grace usually comes in ways we can neither predict nor expect. But also like them, it just might stir our hearts when it does.

17. A Land Between

It's helpful to think about the land of ancient Israel as a "land between," a term coined for the region by the biblical geographer James Monson. How so? The heartland of the biblical story straddles a historic crossroads joining three continents, at a pinch point where the Mediterranean faces the Red Sea. It is, as a result, a homeland wedged between empires, between ecosystems, and between worldviews. This makes the arena of the biblical story a bustling center of activity, but also an active frontier. Egypt, Arabia, Assyria, Babylon, Persia, Greece, and Rome all at one time or another wanted to control this strategic corridor with the goal of expanding their own imperial interests in the region. In the process, as the people of ancient Israel tried to create and maintain their own national and spiritual identity, they were exposed to a wide range of opportunities, challenges, and threats pressing in from the outside. Israel's story, as recorded in the Old and New Testaments, is very much a story of a vulnerable people in a vulnerable land, and of the lessons of grace and faith that ensued.

When we zoom in to the land that fills the space from Dan to Beersheba (1 Kings 4:25), we see a similar pattern, though in miniature. Here are several historic heartlands where, in this case, nation-states (rather than full-blown empires) rose, each separated by lands acting as busy buffers between. To take one example, the heartland of the kingdom of Judah was the high rugged limestone hill country that stretches from just north of its capital city, Jerusalem, to Beersheba. The homeland of one of their most persistent rivals, the Philistines, was the flat, open coastal plain between Joppa (modern Tel Aviv) and Gaza. The latter was open, resourced, and connected; the former rocky, isolated, and relatively poor. The residents of each of these heartlands faced off over a band of low, rounded foothills that served as a buffer—their own land between.

The biblical term for the foothills lying between the Judean highlands and the Philistine coastal plain is *shephelah*, "lowland." Five broad, fertile valleys cut through the *shephelah* on parallel east-

The Sorek Valley stretches toward the coastal plain from the rocky rise of ancient Beth Shemesh. From here, students of the Bible track the story of Samson.

The Elah Valley runs eastward from Khirbet Qeyafa to the rise of the Judean hills, left. Socoh once crowned the low, light green rise opposite. Significant archaeological remains dating to the time of David and Goliath at Qeyafa include this strong gate complex.

west lines, directing water runoff from the highlands to the coast. A number of large, important cities grew up around these valleys in biblical times, including Gezer (1 Kings 9:16–17), Beth Shemesh (2 Kings 14:11), Socoh (1 Sam. 17:1), Azekah (Jer. 34:7), and Lachish (2 Kings 18:14). But most importantly, these *shephelah* valleys served as corridors funneling traffic between the Judean hills and the coast—in biblical times and up until today. We can think of each as a swinging door, opening westward as a strong king in Judah (for instance, Solomon, Jehoshaphat, Uzziah, Hezekiah, or Josiah) tried to tap into the economic opportunities of the coast. More often, though, these doorways swung open the other way, as the Philistines, or later Assyria, Babylon, Greece, and Rome, all pushed inland for conquest, to establish a frontier, to contain Judah, or to dominate trade.

One of these valleys is the Sorek, flowing westward from Beth Shemesh, where Samson, of the tribe of Dan, "loved a [Philistine] woman . . . whose name was Delilah" (Judg. 16:4). The entire Samson drama illustrates the back-and-forth nature of *shephelah*, as Samson and the Philistines took turns chasing each other down at a time when both were trying to establish rights to live in the region (see Judg. 1:34). To the south is the Elah Valley. Here the Philistines under Goliath "gathered their armies for battle . . . at Socoh which belongs to Judah" (1 Sam. 17:1), opening the swinging doors eastward and thwarting Israel's interests in the region in the process. Socoh commanded the direct route between Gath, hometown of Goliath, and Bethlehem. It's no wonder that Jesse sent his sons down to help Saul hold the line (1 Sam. 17:13)!

Three hundred years later, in the days of Hezekiah the king and Isaiah the prophet, the threat from the coast came in the form of the army of Sennacherib, king of Assyria. Sennacherib's eyes were focused on the riches of Egypt, but first he had to contain Judah, and to do that he had to subdue the valleys of the *shephelah*. In the process, he crowed that he had conquered forty-six of Hezekiah's walled forts and strong cities, many of which the Judean king had placed in the corridors of the *shephelah* to try to keep the Assyrians out. Primary among these was Lachish in the southwestern *shephelah*, Judah's most important city after Jerusalem. Isaiah summarized it all this way:

> *Your choicest valleys were full of [Assyrian] chariots, and the horsemen took up fixed positions at the gate. And He removed the defense of Judah.* —Isaiah 22:7–8; see also 2 Chronicles 11:5

This iron "cutout" sculpture depicts a Judean family leaving Lachish by oxcart in advance of the Assyrian attack. Foundational remains of the Judean governor's palace dominate the background.

Scholars have used a variety of descriptive terms to capture the essence of the *shephelah*. It is a "fluid margin," some say, the "shared frontier" of peoples living in the hill country and others out on the coast. It is "debatable ground," open equally to the Judeans and the Philistines. It is a "limin-

al zone" connecting two larger, yet diverse entities. It is a moving "seesaw," with one power up, one power down. It is a precarious "point of balance," often tipped. I like the evocative term "land between." Between what? Between how? The historical and geographical details that have paraded through the valleys of the *shephelah* for millennia amply illustrate the term. At the very least, this is a plot of real estate simultaneously ripe with opportunity and threat. It seems endemic that in a land between— whether it is a local one like the *shephelah* or a larger one such as the entire land of ancient Israel—people live in a perpetual state of uneasy balance: lives that are full yet fragile; tenuous though stable; blessed with resources, blessed without. It is a place where lessons of security and trust are anything but theoretical. If God's word rings true here, it can ring true anywhere. And this, perhaps, is one of the reasons why he chose the land that he did to reveal himself through the all-too-real events of the Bible.

18. A Shepherd's Psalm

We tend to come to the Twenty-Third Psalm with a set of ready-made images in mind. Lush green pastures. Fresh, still waters. A contented shepherd. Plump sheep grazing quietly nearby. Images that come from our own experiences, or Sunday school imaginations. But to be fair to the psalm, we ought to first think of the landscape in which it was composed. Psalm 23 is titled "A Psalm of David." We are not sure if this means it was written by David, written about David, written in memory of David, or written to call David to mind. The idea of David composing songs while following his flocks among the hills is idyllic, but cannot be proven. In any case, we should read the language of Psalm 23 within the backdrop of the dry fields and barren hills east of Bethlehem where David and millennia of shepherds since have grazed their flocks of sheep and goats. Climb up to the top of the Herodium southeast of Bethlehem, or to Mount Scopus northeast of the Old City of Jerusalem. Gaze eastward, out across the wilderness of Judah, erasing all bits of modern infrastructure from your mind as you do. Or, make the winding drive from Jerusalem down to Jericho and stop anywhere within the undulating folds of the rounded hills that tumble into the Wadi Qilt or Wadi Mukallik (Nahal Og). These are our proper visuals for the psalm. This is no easy pasturage, but rather a setting where the climate is unforgiving and ravenous predators abound, a raw arena that mocks attempts at survival training. Yet it is a place where shepherds stay for days, weeks, or even months at a time, living off the land much like their flocks and learning to survive with only what is most necessary for life.

The LORD is my Shepherd, I shall not want.

The psalm's opening affirmation cannot be that [insert your name here] shall not be in want of anything. A proper shepherding context simply doesn't allow this kind of a reading. There's no health and wealth gospel here. Rather, the Lord, my guide, my protector, and my giver of life, will provide everything necessary for life, without

Green pastures in the Judean wilderness.

Water rushing through the Wadi Qilt in the Judean wilderness, running strong after winter rains.

necessarily changing the circumstances in which I am living. I am still grazing the same barren hillsides, looking for patches of green or backwater pools. But my shepherd lives with me, eats with me, lies down with me, gives his everything for me. 24/7. So what else do I need?

He makes me lie down in green pastures.

With chalky hillsides, immature soils, and annual rainfall well below the minimum needed for agriculture, pastures of any kind are few and far between. After a good winter rain, parts of the Judean wilderness do sprout tender grass, but it withers with the heat of the sun after a few short weeks (see Ps. 90:5–6; Isa. 40:7–8). Shepherds learn where patches of grass might remain into the dry summer months; brittle and withered, they can still sustain a flock.

He leads me beside quiet waters. He restores my soul.

The shepherds also know where the springs are—down in the bottom of some of the canyons, running cool and fresh and full of life. But these are few and far between, and a long walk from most of the wilderness hills. Shepherds also know the other kind of water, the flash floods of winter that rend and destroy. With these, the narrow canyon bottoms become places of death; even today, a primary cause of death in the wilderness of Judah is drowning. Useful water is hard to find.

He guides me in the paths of righteousness
for His name's sake.

Paths of righteousness. The right way to walk. In the tangled mass of wilderness hills, the paths to quiet water and green pastures are anything but obvious and can lead to slippery slopes, cliff edges, or the lairs of predators instead. Which is the right way to go? What should I do? It's easy to get lost out here . . .

Without its proper geographical context, the shepherding metaphors of Psalm 23 seem quite pleasant. But now we see that the psalm says more about the shepherd and his keen ability to keep his flock alive than about the land.

Even though I walk through the valley of
the shadow of death ...

Now *that's* a descriptor of the grazing land— and of our situation in life—as it actually is. And that reality usually doesn't change, at least not very much. Yet,

I fear no evil, for You are with me; Your rod and Your staff, they comfort me. You prepare a table before me in the presence of my enemies; You have anointed my head with oil; my cup overflows. Surely goodness and lovingkindness will follow me all the days of my life . . .

An attentive shepherd watches his flock on a rather ragged hillside in Edom.

And now we see the tools and trade of the shepherd: the foremost is being with his sheep, then comes guiding them, correcting them, protecting them, and providing for them. Whatever is good (and that word takes us back to Gen. 1, a descriptor of life the way it's supposed to be) and whatever

makes for lovingkindness (a word that carries connotations of unbreakable covenantal loyalty) follows, like a flock. Like sheep, goodness and lovingkindness become ours.

And I will dwell in the house of the LORD forever.

If David wrote this psalm, the temple in Jerusalem wasn't built yet; indeed, Jerusalem still lay outside of Israelite control. But that doesn't detract from his certainty that the relationship that sheep have with their shepherd, living together as one, is what God desires us to have with him.

19. A River of Life

The wilderness of Judah is a local desert tucked into the rain shadow east of the central hilly spine of Judah. Here rainfall amounts drop as precipitously as does the elevation, from twenty-four inches per year on average on the Mount of Olives to just one-tenth that at the Dead Sea, 4,000 feet below. The soft, chalky hills of the Judean wilderness filling the thirteen-mile-wide band between, barren save for a scant covering of grass on their northern slopes in early spring, are the traditional home of the shepherd. A century ago the historical geographer George Adam Smith called this a "haggard desert," noting its foreboding plunge into the great Jordan Valley beyond.

Over the millennia, heavy rainfall in the hill country of Judah above has eroded the wilderness into a tangled maze of dry watercourses, or *wadis*. All rainfall flowing through these wadis, including runoff into the Kidron that drains Jerusalem eastward, ends up in the Dead Sea, by far the lowest spot and saltiest body of water on earth. The landscape throughout is wild, harsh, and stunning. Without an ongoing source of fresh water, life in the wilderness of Judah is precarious at best. A few perennial springs do flow from the cliff line above the Dead Sea—of these, those at Engedi (see 1 Sam. 24:1) are the best known—but otherwise the Judean wilderness is a dry and thirsty land swallowed by a sterile, salt-encrusted sea.

For the Old Testament residents of Jerusalem living high in the arable hills above, the wilderness of Judah formed a barrier against threats from further east, but was also a reminder that the claws of famine and death always hovered at their door. Beyond the Dead Sea lay Judah's troublesome Transjordanian neighbors, Ammon, Moab, and Edom, and beyond them, a vast stretch of trackless desert into Arabia and Mesopotamia. From these eastern lands came enemies, be it desert raiders intent on plunder (Judg. 6:3–6) or the rolling juggernauts of Assyria and Babylon. Old Testament

With a pungent odor, the Kidron wadi carries large amounts of raw sewage and garbage from the villages east of Jerusalem into the Judean wilderness. Today's reality stands in stark contrast to Ezekiel's image of the Kidron as a river of life.

The Kidron exits the Judean wilderness through this canyon cut on the eastern shore of the Dead Sea, south of Qumran.

Jerusalem withstood all assaults but the last, succumbing in the end to the Babylonians. Nebuchadnezzar's army destroyed Jerusalem and its temple, carrying its best and brightest eastward, across the lifeless wilderness into exile (2 Kings 25).

But these forced refugees didn't leave alone. With a wonderful sense of the geography of his home city, the prophet Ezekiel tells us that as the temple in Jerusalem was about to be overrun, God himself left his earthly abode and went eastward as well, out to the top of the Mount of Olives (Ezek. 9:3; 10:18–19; 11:22–25). From there he could look over the wilderness beyond which the captives of Judah were taken. Did God abandon Israel—or was he exiling himself *with* them?

Later, in his vision of the rebuilt temple, Ezekiel saw God's glory return, retracing its steps back through the barren wilderness of Judah and into the temple (Ezek. 43:1–5). We should note that every time the gospel writers give specific geographical information about how Jesus approached Jerusalem, he is coming from the east (Luke 19:1, 28; John 10:40; 11:7).

God's glory once again filled the temple, but Ezekiel's vision was not over. Now the prophet saw water—divine, living water—flow out of the temple back into the barren, eastern wilderness (Ezek. 47:1–5). Because there is no spring on the temple hill, this was clearly an act of God. Entering the Kidron Valley, the water quickly became a deep river, stronger even than a flash flood caused by heavy rainfall. With language taken directly out of the Genesis creation account, Ezekiel described the miraculous change that overwhelmed the arid wilderness and Dead Sea into which this river flowed:

> Then he said to me, "These waters go out toward the eastern region and go down into the Arabah [the arid shoreline of the Dead Sea]; then they go toward the sea, being made to flow into the sea, and the waters of the sea become fresh. It will come about that every living creature which swarms in every place where the river goes, will live.

And there will be very many fish, for these waters go there and the others become fresh; so everything will live where the river goes. —Ezekiel 47:8–9

As Ezekiel watched, the shoreline between Engedi and Eneglaim, two points defining the southern, saltiest portion of the Dead Sea, were transformed into prime spots for

fishing (Ezek. 47:10), and along the banks of the Kidron, once desolate but now a river of life, grew a garden like Eden (Ezek. 47:7, 12).

What an awesome change for a stark present reality! Does Ezekiel's vision speak about just a geographical spot in Israel, or should we let it inform what can happen to

The Dead Sea, the lowest, saltiest, and most inhumane body of water on earth.

our neighborhoods, wherever they happen to be? Life-giving water, flowing from God into a dry and thirsty land, radically changing everything that it touches for good.

20. A Timely Rhyme

**Signposts:
Jordan River,
Baptismal Site**

History doesn't repeat itself, says an old adage often attributed to Mark Twain, but it does rhyme. Those déjà vu moments, when something from the past echoes into the present, catch us off guard. Given the nature of human behavior, perhaps they shouldn't. In the grand narrative of history, the events coming around again are usually the nasty ones, reruns of the futility of the human endeavor. Same actions, same mistakes, same results. And too often the rhyme is not just "here we go again" but something rather dissonant. When good things rhyme we hardly notice.

The Russian Pilgrimage Residence at Bethany beyond the Jordan, seen from the Israeli security zone west of the Jordan River. The area of green to the right of the building marks the flow of the river; rugged, arid terrain lines both banks.

Japanese congregants and American pilgrims celebrate baptism in the Jordan River at Qasr al-Yahud, on the Israeli (western) side of the river. The eastern bank, in Jordan, lies just a few yards away.

The rhymes that echo down the chambers of history with the clearest sound are those that pair events and place, when repeating *whats* coincide with a *where.* As we read the biblical narrative, we often pay attention to words or themes that we encounter repeatedly in the text. In the process, we would do well to also notice the repetition of *place.* Geographical references are not incidental to the biblical story, but a significant part of it. Understanding them helps us organize events and see something of their significance. The regional location of resources, major routes, entrance and exit points, zones of production, markets, and zones of consumption were all rather stable throughout the biblical period. For this reason, the ebb and flow of events tended to follow somewhat predictable lines. The biblical geographer James Monson rightly speaks about the land of the Bible as a playing board on which the players, that is, the various people and people groups we meet on its pages, took turns moving from here to there. The board doesn't dictate actions, but it certainly influences them, and the pieces sometimes do move in familiar patterns. Reading the Bible and other ancient texts tells us what happened. Understanding the places on the board where events took place helps us better grasp the *hows* and the *whys*.

One of the busiest strategic spots on the playing board of ancient Israel is a confluence of fords that allow travelers to cross the Jordan River north of the Dead Sea. The location coincides with a biblical theme of entering a new place, or a new stage of life. Nowadays this part of the Jordan is the dregs of the river, flowing limpidly only a few yards wide, the water like liquid clay, heavy with agricultural runoff, a dense greenish yellow brown. But travelers to the region 100 years ago report conditions that must have characterized the river from antiquity—fast-moving, often deep, difficult to cross except where the water ran in rapids over rocky shallows. The fords were known crossing points, busy in peacetime, to be seized in battle (Josh. 2:7; Judg. 3:28; 2 Sam. 17:16; 19:15–18; Jer. 51:32). Historically, the Jordan River flooded with the spring rains, the marshy floodplain on either side becoming an impenetrable tangle of scrub growth alive with critters of all kinds, including reptiles and sharp-toothed animals not friendly to humans. The prophet Jeremiah called this the "thicket of the Jordan" and warned of its dangers (Jer. 12:5; 49:19; 50:44). Beyond lies a five-mile run in both directions of some of the most blistered terrain on earth, save for a very few oases such as Jericho. Then the steep rise through the wilderness of Judah westward to Jerusalem, or up to the Gilead and Moabite highlands to the east.

Routes following torturous paths pushed through these barriers, connecting Jerusalem with the capitals of ancient Ammon and Moab to the east, or, in the time of the New Testament, serving as busy gateways on Rome's eastern frontier. More often than not, the Jordan River functioned as a natural eastern border for the land of ancient Israel. Crossing the waters of the Jordan signaled being in the land, or out of it. And, of all of the places where the Jordan could be crossed, it was the fords east of Jericho that carried the rhyme. When we recall that within the biblical narrative east was always the direction of exile and that biblical writers also depicted the appearance of God as an eastern sunrise (Deut. 33:2; Hab. 3:3–4), we have the confluence of some powerfully evocative historical-geographical themes.

Within the biblical story three momentous events track through the channel of the Jordan River north of the Dead Sea. The first was decisive: Joshua brought Israel back home, into their land of promise, though it first had to be conquered. (Josh. 3:1–4:14). The second was pivotal:

Elijah, a prophet who "felt fiercely" (in the words of Abraham Heschel), left the land of promise—and with it the confines of earth—by crossing the Jordan eastward. His doubly endowed disciple Elisha returned like Joshua, to hearts that needed to be conquered (2 Kings 2:1–14). The third, of course, is the baptism of Jesus, an expectant moment culminating in a rhyme as clear as can be. John the Baptist, with prophetic garb and commanding speech reminiscent of Elijah, chose this spot busy with historic associations to call his people to an uncomfortable account. Born into the Jerusalem priesthood (see Luke 1:5–25, 57–66), the Baptist was drawn to the Jordan where, like Joshua and Elisha, he said, "Let's begin anew."

A Russian Orthodox pilgrim rises from the waters of baptism in the Jordan River.

Now in those days John the Baptist came,
preaching in the wilderness of Judea, saying,
"Repent, for the kingdom of heaven is at
hand."... Now John himself had a garment
of camel's hair and a leather belt around his
waist; his food was locusts and wild honey.
Then Jerusalem was going out to him, and
all Judea and all the district around the
Jordan; and they were being baptized by
him in the Jordan River, as they
confessed their sins.

—Matthew 3:1–2, 4–6

Today, traditional sites of Jesus' baptism face off against each other, one in the wilderness of Judea (Matt. 3:1–6), the other across the Jordan River (John 1:28) just yards away. Pilgrims greet each other across the watery divide. Many reenact Jesus' baptism (just don't ingest the water!), and the Israeli National Park Service ensures that white doves are always around to fly by. Each visitor has to decide for themselves whether it's all devotionally appropriate, or a bit too much. But what is certain is that down here—through a landscape that is otherwise stark, dangerous, and devoid of helpful life—runs a river of life, and in its water Jesus began a life journey by which all things become new.

21. A Study in Grace

Jericho. A place with a famous name, and justifiably so. As near as we can tell from archaeology, the mound of Jericho (Tell es-Sultan) deserves the title "Oldest City on Earth," with evidence that it was a walled center long before even the invention of pottery. It also proudly carries the title "Lowest City on Earth," ringing in at 850 feet below sea level, three times lower than Death Valley, California. And it is a true oasis, watered by a spring that flows throughout the year at an average rate of 1,000 gallons per minute, giving Jericho the nickname "city of palm trees" (Deut. 34:3; Judg. 3:13). Other springs, at Na'aran just to the north and in

Modern Jericho, still the "city of palm trees."

121

A portion of the bath complex at the Jericho palace of Herod the Great. The peak behind was crowned with a fortress that guarded the site, which Herod named Cypros, after his mother. The road to Jerusalem tracked through the line of trees between.

the Wadi Qilt a mile south, add water to the region, bringing perennial green to what is otherwise "a land of salt without inhabitant" (Jer. 17:6). The first-century-AD historian Josephus called Jericho "that most favored spot" (*Jewish War* 4.474).

But in the flow of human history, perhaps the most significant thing about the location of Jericho is not these geographic wonders but rather the city's position as a gateway first into Canaan, and then into the land of ancient Israel, from the east. With the Dead Sea blocking easy east-west traffic on the south, the Jericho oasis became the magnet for traffic moving between Transjordan and Jerusalem. This was Joshua's entrance on his way to divide and conquer Canaan (Josh. 5–6). During the time of the judges, Jericho was Moab's launchpad to do the same (Judg. 3:12–30), with Ahab, in the ninth century BC, turning the tables as he pushed through the gateway city of Jericho to conquer Moab (1 Kings 16:33–34; 2 Kings 1:1). And of course this was where Elisha crossed back into Israel having received the prophetic mantle from Elijah, following the track of Joshua where, rather than conquering Jericho, Elisha cured its water and restored life to its people (2 Kings 2:1–22).

By the time of the New Testament, the main activity at Jericho had moved about a mile south, from the mound of Tell es-Sultan to the banks of the Wadi Qilt, a huge drainage system that channels spring water and seasonal rainwater from the Judean hills down into the Jordan Valley. In the late second century BC, the Hasmonean (Maccabean) royal family built a sumptuous palace here, where they controlled the route that rose to Jerusalem on a ridge just west of the site. Travelers have walked this Jericho road for millennia; over the past century, parts have been improved for vehicle traffic.

In the decades before the birth of Jesus, Herod the Great supersized the Hasmonean palace at Jericho by building three separate palaces at the site, replete with variegated tile floors, frescoed walls, columned reception halls, dining halls, bath houses, swimming pools, fountains, a garden with planted and potted plants, and other accoutrements fit for anyone whose epithet was "the Great." Herod placed his most elegant structures on the northern bank of the wadi. These were joined to those on the southern side with a bridge, the first ever built in the land. Herod directed fresh spring water to his baths and pools through a nine-mile-long aqueduct that serviced his palaces year-round. Here Rome's appointed tyrant could escape the winter chill of Jerusalem while banqueting in decadent splendor, with one eye on the wealth of the Arabian spice route that entered the Roman Empire through Jericho, the other closed to the desperate struggles of the Jews he had been enthroned to rule. By the time of Jesus' adult ministry, control of Jericho had passed to Pontius Pilate, the Roman prefect of Judea, with the same endgame.

What kind of people might we expect to find here? In the Gospels we meet two by name, blind Bartimaeus and the tax collector Zaccheus (Mark 10:46–52; Luke 18:35–19:10). Jesus encountered both on his last trip to Jerusalem, where he was to celebrate Passover and await the cross. They represent two types of people we would expect to find on the margins of a place of great wealth. Bartimaeus was a man beaten down by life, reduced to begging, his physical handicap likely a cause. With a good Aramaic name we can assume he was Jewish, but apparently ostracized from his support group and left to fend—loudly, we read (Luke 18:38–39)—for himself. Jericho was a gateway on a road well traveled by people of means, and Bartimaeus hoped to benefit from their trickle-down economy. He wanted mercy, and so identified Jesus as the Son of David, recognizing Jesus' superior position and imploring him to fulfill the role of the ideal king whose responsibility from of old was to help those who could neither provide for nor protect themselves. We note Psalm 82:3–4:

> *Vindicate the weak and fatherless; do justice to the afflicted and destitute. Rescue the weak and needy; deliver them out of the hand of the wicked.*

For today's young residents of Jericho, the ruins of Herod's palace are a playground. Herod once played here, too.

What Bartimaeus received was grace: his sight, and a purpose and means for living.

Zaccheus stands on the other end of the socioeconomic spectrum. He, too, was apparently Jewish, based on his name (Zaccheus is the Greek form of the Hebrew name Zakkai, which means, ironically, "the pure one"), but was also a collector of taxes for the foreign occupying power. And there was a lot of wealth passing through Jericho to be taxed, from

Arabian spices to balsam (the world's supply grew along the Dead Sea between Jericho and Engedi) to a tax on everyone crossing the border to or from Transjordan (Perea). Zaccheus certainly made full use of his position to extort, enriching himself on the backs of his own countrymen. His later confession, "If I have defrauded anyone," was likely a face-saving admission of guilt, one that Jesus accepted with grace (Luke 19:8).

Two people we meet by name. One was an expendable, the other a collaborator. Were they candidates to be followers—disciples—of Jesus? We might not think so, but given Jesus' practice of extending grace, they absolutely were. If they (read: we) had somehow deserved or earned the right to follow Jesus, then his response wouldn't have been grace.

Bartimaeus followed Jesus on the road (Mark 10:52); Zaccheus likely did as well, probably letting someone else tend the shop for a while. So we might reasonably expect to find them walking with Jesus up to Jerusalem. It was, after all, nearly Passover, a festival worth celebrating. If so, did they witness Jesus' triumphal entry? His crucifixion? And later, his ascension? Most of the people whom Jesus encountered or healed remain forever anonymous—but we know the names of these two. This has prompted some scholars to suggest that Bartimaeus and Zaccheus became leaders in the church, despite their less than perfect beginnings.

Would I be able to accept people like Zaccheus and Bartimaeus as leaders in my church? Usually, I want people to extend grace to me, but don't necessarily want to offer it to others. Gracefully, Jesus extends it differently.

22. Questing and Dwelling

The excavated site of Tel Beersheba is a feast for archaeological eyes. The excavation team, led by Yohanan Aharoni of Tel Aviv University in the 1970s, was guided by the principle that large sections of the mound should be uncovered in order to provide a wide understanding of what an urban center from the time of the Judean monarchy looked like. Because much of what Aharoni's team excavated has been partially reconstructed, visitors to the site today are able to see actual living spaces of Iron Age Judah without too much difficulty. The excavated remains include a city wall and gate complex, two water collection systems, warehouses, a religious center, a piazza, a governor's residence, and private housing, all organized in a sophisticated city plan. From this, we can posit that Beersheba functioned as an economic hub and gateway on Judah's southern frontier for nearly half a millennium (see 1 Kings 4:25; 2 Kings 23:8). And because the city was located in a part of the Negev that otherwise was too dry for permanent settlement, it was likely supported and supplied by a government in Jerusalem that sought to ensure its own long-term viability in the region.

Yet the Beersheba that most Bible readers know was something quite different. This was the Beersheba of Abraham, Isaac, and Jacob (Gen. 21:22–34; 26:26–33; 28:10), a place with only a goat-hair tent, a tamarisk tree, and a well (Gen. 21:30, 33). Of these, only the well might be archaeologically recoverable, and one was, just outside the gate of Iron Age Beersheba, though it does not date to the time of the patriarchs. Because the soil in this part of the Negev is soft and powdery and the water table relatively close to the surface of the ground, we can assume that a number of wells were dug in the vicinity of ancient Beersheba at any given time in history. Some are known to archaeologists; most, long ago filled in, never will be. It is largely for this reason that the location of the Beersheba of the patriarchs cannot be marked with an X on the ground. At best, we can imagine its existence by gazing across the Negev horizon while standing on the heavy iron observation deck that now crowns the mound of the ancient Judean site.

The archaeological remains at Tel Beersheba date to the Iron Age, the time of the Judean monarchy. Here students of biblical archaeology view the remains of houses that formed the perimeter of the ancient site.

The narrative line of the biblical patriarchs is familiar. It begins with God's call to the shepherding seminomad Abram—later renamed Abraham—to move from Harran in northwestern Mesopotamia to a place he did not yet know:

Questing.
Dwelling.
Abraham's search
for a home took
him to Beersheba
and beyond.

Now the LORD said to Abram, "Go forth
from your country, and from your relatives,
and from your father's house, to the land
which I will show you . . ."

—Genesis 12:1

Abraham's travels, and those of his son Isaac and grandson Jacob, are consistent with what we know of the patterned movements of seminomads in the ancient Near East throughout history, a practice that has persisted in parts of the Middle East up until the recent past. Following the change of seasons in search of water and grass, these shepherd herders would move into semiarid steppe lands bordering the North Arabian Desert when winter rains converted the gasping ground into grazing land, then

The well and watering trough at Tel Beersheba stand just outside the city gate, both nicely reconstructed by Israel's Antiquities Authority and National Park Service. Though dating to the time of the Judean monarchy, they provide a nice visual for stories of the patriarchs that took place at wells.

migrate back toward familiar hillier areas north and west during the rainless summer, where water resources remained accessible. In the process, and especially in times of famine, these shepherd herders came into frequent and persistent contact with people living in cities that lay on the seam where the steppe lands meet the hills. There the shepherds would trade resources and enter into long-term, protective relationships with the rulers of the city. Usually shepherd herders would maintain contact with their original home base, even if they ended up settling in the vicinity of other urban areas. So we see Abraham, Isaac, and Jacob settling for periods of time near the Canaanite cities of Shechem, Bethel, Hebron, and Gerar

(Gen. 12:6–8; 13:3; 18:1; 20:1; 23:19; 26:1; 28:19; 33:18; 35:1; 37:12), places with resources they kept coming back to, yet returning to Harran to strengthen their own interfamily ties (Gen. 24:1–4; 28:1–5, 10). Their interpersonal relationships with the people in these cities were sometimes cooperative, sometimes rocky, and sometimes, at least to our eyes, a bit scandalous.

Reflecting on this lifestyle, the writer of the book of Hebrews notes that the journeys of the patriarchs were also journeys of faith, a kind of interplay of questing and dwelling, a back-and-forth search for security and arrival in places where life just wasn't yet right.

> *Not knowing where [they were] going . . .*
> *liv[ing] as an alien in the land of promise,*
> *as in a foreign land, dwelling in tents . . .*
> *looking for the city which has foundations,*
> *whose architect and builder is God.*
>
> —Hebrews 11:8–10

In the book of Hebrews, the goal is a heavenly city, a place of eternal security and rest. But the underlying context is the kind of place where shepherd herders needed to settle for provision and protection, fully recognizing that their own resource base was never quite adequate.

And so our lives, too, are journeys of questing and dwelling. We search for meaning where it's obscure, for answers to questions that we don't even quite know how to ask yet, for security in our physical and psychological and spiritual beings. That's questing. Dwelling is deepening who we already are, drawing from the rich set of resources that only the Lord God of life can provide. Questing and dwelling are neither a one-and-done sequence nor an either/or. Rather, they are both/and, part of a lifelong process through which God strengthens our inmost beings. Embracing the value of dwelling and of questing, we can be confident that our quests do lead us home.

23. This Is Sinai

Signposts:
Egypt,
Mount Sinai

South of the wide sand sheet that lines the Mediterranean Sea, south of the horizonless limestone interior called *et-Tih*, "the one who is lost," and south of the Mars-scape-red sandstone hills beyond, are the wrinkled granite mountains that fill the southern tip of the Sinai Peninsula. From the middle of this jumbled mass of hoary bedrock rises Jebel Musa, Moses' Mountain, a place identified by Byzantine monks in the early fourth century AD as Mount Sinai.

It has become fashionable to discount Jebel Musa's authenticity in favor of another mountain—dozens of other mountains, to be precise—found in other parts of the

Sunrise from Jebel Musa, Mount Sinai.

Saint Catherine's Monastery at the base of Jebel Musa, the repository of some of the oldest patterns of Christianity in the Middle East.

Sinai Peninsula, Israel's Negev, Saudi Arabia, or the Hashemite Kingdom of Jordan. Amid this academic and quasi-academic noise the merits of the traditional site remain strong. A location in southern Sinai is consistent with God's command that Moses avoid the northern coastal route, "the way of the land of the Philistines" (Ex. 13:17). There are a number of permanent small springs in the vicinity of Jebel Musa, marking it as among the most reliable spots for fresh water anywhere in the peninsula and a natural draw for a multitude passing through. The broad Plain of Rahah ("Rest") about a mile northwest of Jebel Musa was large enough for

Israel's encampment before the mountain (Ex. 19:2); it is the location of a number of tourist hotels today. And, perhaps most notably, a host of ancient Greek and Latin sources (Herodotus *Histories* 2.12; Strabo *Geography* 17.1.21; Polyaenus *Stratagems in War* 7.2.7; Aelius Aristides *Orations* 36, 87; Basil of Caesarea *Hexameron* 4, p. 29, col 88; etc.) agree that the regional term Arabia included all or part of the Sinai Peninsula, as required by Galatians 4:25: "Now this Hagar is Mount Sinai in Arabia . . ." At 7,497 feet, Jebel Musa is not the tallest mountain in the area; that honor belongs to the 8,652-foot Jebel Katherina off its southern flank, the highest peak in all of Egypt. But we must recall that nothing in the exodus account requires that Mount Sinai be the highest, and Jebel Katherina lacks the specific physical requirements that are present on and around Jebel Musa anyway.

Because Jebel Musa fits all the necessary prerequisites to be Mount Sinai, nothing disqualifies it from being the best candidate for the site. On the other hand, this doesn't prove the accuracy of the location either. Still, there is no a priori reason to think that the early Byzantine memory was wrong; after all, they, too, matched the place with the data of the biblical text and knew good and well that in their day, southern Sinai was part of Arabia. The Greek Orthodox monks, heirs of the Byzantine tradition, persist within the walled compound of St. Catherine's Monastery at the northern base of the mountain. Here visitors can witness the spirit of some of the earliest expressions of Christianity in the Middle East. This alone is worth pilgrimage to the site.

The rising sun warms expectant pilgrims huddled atop Jebel Musa.

Irrespective of the accuracy of its physical location, Mount Sinai towers over the biblical landscape. Here, in an awesome yet personal encounter, God gave Torah, literally "instruction," through which ancient Israel was to understand their relationship with him and each other. The mountain casts a long shadow over subsequent Jewish, Christian, and Islamic history as well. *Moses.* Hebrew *Moshe.* Arabic *Musa.* The presence of this indomitable man of God has indeed shaped human history.

Over the years I have climbed Mount Sinai with students or family more than a dozen times—OK, once in a while on camelback. We usually start at a frigid 2:00 a.m. so that we can reach the summit to see the sun rise over the Arabian Peninsula's Hijaz Mountains. Sometimes we hike under the brightness of a full moon and experience the powerful effect that "the lesser light to govern the night" (Gen. 1:16) has on people living in the open desert. Sometimes we are enveloped by a pitch-black sky punctuated with so many stars that they are impossible to count (see Gen. 15:5). And once, a thunderstorm had just passed through, with lightning leaping from low-hanging clouds across the southeastern horizon.

O God, when You went forth before Your
people, when You marched through the
wilderness, the earth quaked; the heavens
also dropped rain at the presence of God;
Sinai itself quaked at the presence of God,
the God of Israel.

—Psalm 68:7–8; see also Judges 5:4–5

The descriptions of Mount Sinai as viewed by Israel camped at its base include language that resembles an earthquake, a thunderstorm, and a volcano (Ex. 19:18). Perhaps all are attempts to describe something so awesome, so much beyond prior human experience, that the moment could be depicted no other way.

Nowadays people journey to Mount Sinai out of curiosity, because it's a tourist attraction, or for its educational or spiritual value. Many, though, are still drawn to the mountain to get away from all manner of life conditions and find out who God really is. Perhaps this was Elijah's motive as he fled Jezebel to encounter God as a still, small voice (1 Kings 19:1–13). But neither Moses, nor all Israel, nor Elijah lingered on the mountain. Having been transformed, they descended the mount and walked back into the real world.

I no longer walk up and down Mount Sinai as fast as I used to. On one of our most recent sunrise visits, my wife and I were among the last to descend, feeling each stone step deliberately as we slowly made our way. Not far below the summit, three younger and much more agile men who had made the journey from Bangladesh overtook us. Smiling, one of them said, "We want to help you. It's part of human." Indeed. The divine-human encounter at Mount Sinai was an infusion of God's character into people, into us. And it's the kind of encounter that, when accepted, transforms others, and the world, one person at a time.

24. The Sanctuary

Signposts:
Shiloh

The books of Joshua and Judges recount stories of how Israel entered not just a new land, but a new stage in life. The Israelites had lived in Egypt for centuries, but it was never home. For a generation they had wandered "like sheep . . . in the wilderness" (Ps. 78:52), across "a howling waste of a wilderness" (Deut. 32:10), through "a land of drought and deep darkness" (Jer. 2:6), managing their time not so willingly but, we might imagine, eventually finding its rhythm. Then into Canaan, "a land of hills and valleys that drinks water from the rain of heaven, a land for which the LORD our God cares" (Deut. 11:11–12). Canaan was to be their

Ancient Shiloh, the long, exposed mound in the center of the picture, was nestled among the hills of Ephraim. Many scholars think that the location of the tabernacle was on the far right (northern) side of the site.

These thin walls were once part of buildings dating to the early Iron Age, the time of the events of Judges and 1 Samuel.

home, but it was not empty of people nor in any case a land where life would be easy. So Joshua encouraged his fellow Israelites as together they poised for a new beginning:

"Be strong and courageous. Do not tremble or be dismayed, for the LORD your God is with you wherever you go."

—Joshua 1:9

Israel's first religious and political center was Shiloh. It remains a beautiful setting, especially in springtime, crowning a low rise nestled in the Ephraimite hills. The site is hidden between the higher hills of the watershed ridge, which form a sweeping arc to the east, and the main natural route connecting Bethel with Shechem (modern Ramallah with Nablus) via Lebonah to the west. Ancient Shiloh was not visible from either; in fact, the author of Judges had to give off-road directions to the place, apparently under the assumption that most of his readers later in the biblical period wouldn't have known where it was (Judg. 21:19). Today the primary north-south route, Israeli Highway 60, bends to connect Shiloh with the main flow of vehicular traffic through the region, but this is incidental to the biblical story. Well-watered and with a pleasant climate, the broad valleys surrounding Shiloh are more than adequate to provide everything for a healthy, full diet. We read, for instance, of an annual grape harvest festival in Shiloh during the time of the judges (Judg. 21:19). While not specifically named, it was a feast (Heb. *hag*, "pilgrimage festival") that seems to have mirrored, at least in intent, the Feast of Booths (Heb. *hag sukkot*) marking the ingathering of summer fruit in early autumn (Ex. 23:16; Deut. 16:13–15).

The tabernacle was in Shiloh in those early days (Josh. 18:1); exactly where we are not sure. On the strength of an early church tradition, some scholars suggest it was just off the southern end of the mound where four basilicas were built in the Byzantine period. Others prefer the crest of the hill, where a garish visitors' center now stands, since sacred precincts often crowned the highest point of a site. Most, however, including the custodians of the site today, prefer a location on the site's northern slope, a worked bedrock scarp on an east-west axis (Ex. 26:22) nearly the same dimensions as the tabernacle. Unfortunately, there will likely never be enough evidence to make a definitive decision.

In any case, biblical Shiloh itself was a sanctuary in the most real sense of the word. Here Israel could settle down quietly and securely, find itself, and start to grow, out of the way of the hustle and bustle of the remnant of old Canaanite centers that still dotted the landscape. Its most remarkable resident was Samuel, a small-town boy who hailed from Ramathaim (1 Sam. 1:1), a village half a day's walk south. When he was still quite young, Samuel's parents, Hannah and Elkanah, entrusted the lad to the high priest Eli, whose relationship with his own boys was questionable at best (1 Sam. 2:12–36). These were difficult times, with prophecy—clear direction for life from God—infrequent (1 Sam. 3:1). Based on the archaeological record, the overall economy was relatively poor as well, with the biblical account adding the recurring threat of invasion and, if that wasn't trouble enough, the fact that pretty much everyone did whatever he or she saw fit (Judg. 21:25). Israel needed vision, and direction, indeed.

"And the LORD appeared again at Shiloh," in the tabernacle, the "dwelling place" of God (1 Sam. 3:21). The book of Exodus provides additional names for the structure, calling it the "sanctuary" and "the tent of meeting" (Ex. 25:8–9; 27:21). The tabernacle was a holy place, where God could be encountered. It was erected at Shiloh (Josh. 18:1), a place which itself was a sanctuary. And it was here that Samuel listened. "Here I am," he said, then "Speak, for Your servant is listening" (1 Sam. 3:4, 10). God revealed himself to Samuel in the quietness of the

night, in an intensely personal moment, in deeply troubling times. It was a life direction moment, one of those times when Samuel just knew. And, armed with God-given confidence, he called to a rough and tumble world.

The February blossoms of an almond tree at Shiloh, a harbinger of spring and the beginning of something new.

25. Full Circle

On one of those fine early autumn days when the sea winds of the Mediterranean push over the landscape of the Bible, carrying billowing white clouds that sweep the summer haze from the sky, we can do no better than to drive, walk, or climb to the top of the closest high hill and have a look around. On days like these, ridge lines and vales, stands of trees and towers (all many miles away and blurred for months by the pale gray skies of summer), suddenly reappear, sharp and clear and somehow close by—and with them emerges an awareness of just how compact the land of ancient Israel actually is.

One such hill, upon whose rounded summit every reader of the Bible should stand on a day of clear horizons, is Mount Gerizim. It's one of those full-circle views. Out to the west the landscape curves downward to the coast, with bustling cities dotting a wide plain that fronts the Mediterranean. To the east, the eye takes in the rise of the hills of Gilead out over the Jordan Valley rift. Though the view north is largely blocked by Mount Ebal, Gerizim's higher twin (access to the top of *that* mountain is restricted by an army base), over Ebal's left shoulder are the hills of Nazareth and over its right shoulder those of the Golan Heights rising to the slopes of Mount Hermon, some seventy-five miles away. To the south, the hills of Ephraim bound away to the bump of Nabi Samwil, from whose top an equally fine view takes in Jerusalem and Judea. At the base of Gerizim, east and north, lies a junction of broad, fertile valleys all converging on the ancient site of Shechem, with Sychar nearby.

It is the hill country of Ephraim and Manasseh, the hills and vales of the close horizon (when viewed from Gerizim), that commands the closest geographical attention. With it a long line of familiar events parades off the pages of the Bible. When Abraham came into the land of Canaan, his first stop, where he built an altar and heard the voice of the Lord, was at the oak of

Mount Gerizim, seen from the remains of Canaanite Shechem.

Moreh just outside Shechem (Gen. 12:6–7). When Joshua brought the sons of Israel back across the Jordan to ratify the covenant of Sinai in their old/new homeland, the blessings of a full life in an equally blessed land were first spoken from the slopes of Mount Gerizim (Deut. 11:29; Josh. 8:30–35). It was to Shechem that Joshua called all Israel to witness his last will and testament and echo the commitment that "as for me and my house, we will serve the LORD" (Josh. 24:1–18). And the ark of the covenant, that tangible object that was a reminder of the reality of Immanuel, God-with-us, rested first at Shiloh, a place nestled in the Ephraim hills not too far to the south (Josh. 18:1; 1 Sam. 1:3). God had promised to give Israel a land (Ex. 12:25) and to care for them once they settled in it (Deut. 11:12). That promise was strong, with the expectation that a life rooted under what Jacob described as the "blessings of heaven above . . . of the deep that lies beneath . . . up to the utmost bound of the everlasting hills" (Gen. 49:25–26) could only leave a legacy of life the way it was

A Samaritan priest with a scroll containing the Samaritan Pentateuch, the sect's holy book.

supposed to be. But of course the biblical account of the history of the tribes of Ephraim and Manasseh, then that of the northern kingdom of Israel, and finally that of the Samaritans, each of whom in turn considered these hills to be their home, shows otherwise. Once blessed, their fall from grace was far.

The tendency of Bible readers is to focus in the end on the grace that was given Jerusalem, the holy city, and the Davidic line from which Messiah would come. And from Jerusalem the gospel did spring. Though spoken in the towns and villages from Nazareth to Capernaum and on the shore of the Sea of Galilee, though anticipated among the fields "white for harvest" near Sychar (John 4:35) and by the actions of the good Samaritan (Luke 10:30–37), it was in Jerusalem that redemption finally had its say. And then, on the slopes of the Mount of Olives overlooking that city, the risen Jesus commanded his followers to be his witnesses "even to the remotest part of the earth" (Acts 1:8). But first they were to go to Samaria, and one of them, Philip, did, bringing

This well, now in a grotto under the Greek Orthodox church at Sychar, has been remembered from the Byzantine period as the well at which Jesus met the woman. Its name, Jacob's Well, comes from John 4:6.

Students of the Bible take in the eastward view above the remains of the Byzantine church Mary Theotokos atop Mount Gerizim. The ancient Samaritan temple likely was in the same location.

back a report that people living in the hills where the work of God had first begun had responded to his new work in Jesus. And with it, the good news of God's blessing had come full circle—and from it, the gospel could flow out of a hilly heartland to a world beyond. The apostle Paul, a come-lately follower of Jesus who made "the remotest part of the earth" his mission field, perhaps said it best (he said a lot of things best):

For I am confident of this very thing, that
He who began a good work in you will
perfect it until the day of Christ Jesus.

—Philippians 1:6

God was faithful to his promise. To a people, yes, but to individual people as well. It started with the sovereignty of God, and that's where it ends. Around that full circle he has plenty of opportunities to show people who they are and make them into what he wants them to be—sometimes in spite of us but preferably as God-with-us.

26. It Comes with Privilege

Ahab and Jezebel. Now there's a power couple, for better or for worse. While the biblical writers emphasized the worse—and for good reason—we shouldn't overlook the better if we want to understand something about the context in which they lived.

Building on the accomplishments of his father, Omri, Ahab was, in the raw arena of geopolitics, actually rather successful. Omri, who was commander of the Israelite army, had seized the Israelite throne in a coup d'état while fighting a battle to expand Israel's interests on the coast (1 Kings 16:15–23). Ambitious and designing, he curtailed Judah in the process. Omri then conquered and occupied the kingdom of Moab east of the Dead Sea. Having seized control of the valuable trades routes approaching his kingdom from the southwest (Egypt) and southeast (Arabia), Omri next brought Phoenicia, lord of the Mediterranean's sea lanes, into his orbit through a trade alliance, sealing the deal by marriage: the Phoenician princess Jezebel became the wife of Ahab, the Israelite crown prince. And to reap the profit from these moves, Omri relocated the Israelite capital from Tirzah, a city hidden in the east Manasseh hills, to Samaria, a commanding site in a picturesque valley overlooking his gateway to the coast (1 Kings 16:24). Then he died.

Ahab inherited a robust and expanding kingdom that was well on the way to duplicating the golden age of David and Solomon. He promptly set his eyes on Aram (in modern-day Syria) and the northeast, the only quadrant of the land not yet under Israelite control. To facilitate his effort, Ahab established a secondary capital at Jezreel. This was a site well suited for his goals. It was a short day's walk due north of his primary capital at Samaria, allowing quick communication with headquarters, and it commanded the narrow neck of the Jezreel Valley at a point only a mile from the southernmost edge of the Galilee hills. From here, Ahab could control the flow of international traffic moving east-west across his kingdom, keep a watchful eye on what was happening in Galilee, and aim his intentions toward Syria.

Ancient Jezreel, now a cattle pasture but open to visitors searching for the memory of Ahab and Jezebel.

The city of Jezreel, which became Ahab's main chariot base, was such a dominant point of control that it gave its name to the entire valley it overlooked.

Archaeologists have uncovered a large, rectangular fortification that dominated the top of the hill on which Jezreel was built, dating to the time of Ahab, the ninth century BC. With towers on each of its four corners and surrounded by a moat, the fortress was massive, enclosing eleven acres. The main gate faced south, toward Samaria. The spring serving the fortress was halfway downslope to the east, today still flowing and easily identified by a tall stand of eucalyptus trees. A horizon-line view from the crest of the hill on which Ahab's fort at Jezreel was built takes in the direct route to Samaria southward, Mount Carmel to the west, the Galilee hills rising to the north, and Gilead (in Transjordan) to the east, all forming a perimeter around the international zone that was the Jezreel Valley. We can imagine Ahab standing on one of the towers of his royal residence and taking in the incredible view of his kingdom.

We can also easily posit that Ahab controlled (let's say "owned" by royal prerogative) not only the perimeter of the fortified site, but also the spring and a strip of land connecting the two. There was already a village on the hill when he chose it for the location of his fortified palace, inhabited by people whose families had lived off the land for generations. One such family was Naboth's, whose ancestral land was near Ahab's pal-

ace (1 Kings 21:2). Soil analysis shows that the soils on the eastern slope facing the spring are best suited for growing grapes while those to the west are better suited for olives, so perhaps Naboth's land was on the eastern side of the mound. The current dig directors, Drs. Norma Franklin and Jennie Ebeling, have also found treading floors and rock-cut vats on the eastern slope, in the direction of the spring, all supporting the general tenor of the Naboth story.

We cannot overestimate the importance of ancestral land in ancient Israel and the right of individual families to live quiet, productive

The view eastward from the mound of Jezreel. It was in this direction that Ahab set his eyes in chariot battle against the Syrians, his persistent Transjordanian neighbor to the northeast.

The spring of
Jezreel is in
the stand of
eucalpytus trees
seen here from
the eastern edge
of the mound
of Jezreel.
The fertile
field between
supported
vineyards in the
days of Naboth
and Ahab.

lives each under their own vine and fig tree (see 1 Kings 4:25). This was the ideal, protected by custom and an ethos that had its roots in the value of individual lives embedded in the law of Moses. To give up one's ancestral land was to choose exile over identity, a self-immolation of belonging and place. As king, Ahab was supposed to respect and protect these rights. But for him, the realities of life—his royal life—were more important. Whatever scruples he had were quickly swept aside when Jezebel reminded him he *was* king, after all, and then concocted a crime to do Naboth in that had the appearance of legality (1 Kings 21:3–14).

The story of Ahab and Naboth is a kind of Cain-and-Abel story, the sin of killing to take

(Gen. 4:1–15). In the end, was Ahab really so different from us? He was in a privileged position, but even those of us with much less privilege can take advantage of others. And in our age of shades of gray, there are so many ways to get to what we want without shedding blood.

It took a prophet, Elijah, to call Ahab to account:

> *"Thus says the LORD: 'Have you murdered and also taken possession?'"*
>
> —1 Kings 21:19

The biblical prophets were unique in the ancient world, and all too infrequent in ours. According to Abraham Heschel, "the prophet is a man who feels fiercely," with prophecy being "the voice that God has lent to the silent agony, a voice to the plundered poor, to the profaned riches of the world. It is a form of living, a crossing point of God and man" (*The Prophets*, 5). And perhaps most tragic is that the prophets were nearly always unwelcome among their own people (see Luke 4:24).

Prophets are good to have around to check certain personal or social excesses, but they're only taken seriously if they criticize the same things that the majority already say need criticizing. Like Ahab in the Old Testament and the people of Nazareth in the New, most of us are not ready to recognize, much less be challenged by, any prophets in our midst.

27. Revisited

The fertile Jezreel Valley, which is shaped like a broad arrowhead thrust toward Mount Carmel and the Mediterranean Sea, separates the hill country of Israel from the hills of Galilee to the north. The Jezreel Valley is connected to the Jordan River by a long, narrow shaft called the Harod Valley. They join at the base of the "arrowhead." Mount Moreh, a 1,700-foot-high rise of soft limestone with a black basalt cap, looms over this juncture, providing a lofty view of the valley floors below.

During the time of the Old Testament, the town of Shunem stood at this point, clinging to the southwestern slopes of Mount Moreh. Blessed with a pleasant climate, fertile soil, an abundance of good building materials, and several large springs, Shunem had every natural advantage to ensure its inhabitants a good life. The men and women of Shunem farmed the grain fields of the Jezreel and Harod Valleys, reaping the harvest of their efforts every spring, after the end of the rainy season.

A busy international highway ran alongside Shunem, hugging the edge of the Harod and Jezreel Valleys. This highway connected points in Transjordan with the Mediterranean coast via the strategic gateway city of Beth Shan at the very eastern end of the Harod Valley "shaft." Elisha, who hailed from Abel Meholah just south of Beth Shan (1 Kings 19:16), would have walked this route whenever he traveled to Mount Carmel (see 2 Kings 2:25; 4:25). Shunem lay exactly at the midpoint of his journey, making it a convenient resting spot for the prophet. From the account of Elisha's life recorded in the book of 2 Kings, we can assume that he also stopped at other towns and villages along the way, ministering to people whenever he had a chance. In this way Elisha foreshadowed Jesus, who also "went about doing good" (Acts 10:38).

The story of Elisha and the woman from Shunem is one of the better known stories of the Old Testament (2 Kings 4:8–37). The Shunammite and her husband, a prosperous yet childless couple, built a rooftop guest room for Elisha to use whenever he passed by. Out of gratitude, Elisha announced that the woman would have a son. Tragically, the

The low shoulder of Mount Moreh, with the village of Sulam, ancient Shunem, edging the valley at its base. The soil stretching into the valley is some of the best in the entire country—which explains why every time Shunem appears in ancient sources, its fields and crops are mentioned. The view is from Jezreel, northward.

The village of Nein, ancient Nain, is the scattering of houses climbing the slope of Mount Moreh in the distance, here pointed out from the Nazareth Ridge.

young child died while helping his father harvest the wheat fields in the heat of early summer, apparently a victim of sunstroke. Elisha responded as only a prophet of God could: in a tender moment infused with divine power, he raised the boy to life.

By the time of the New Testament, the village of Shunem was no more. People still lived on Mount Moreh, but the center of village life had shifted from the southwestern to the northern slope of the hill, to a village called Nain. No doubt the people of Nain remembered Elisha, the great prophet who had visited their ancestors on Mount Moreh over eight centuries before, going about doing good. The story of Elisha and the Shunammite woman must have been handed down among the people of Shunem—and then Nain—from generation to generation, giving a sense of divine identity to the two towns.

Then, one day, history repeated itself—only better.

> *Soon afterwards He went to a city called Nain; and His disciples were going along with Him, accompanied by a large crowd. Now as He approached the gate of the city, a dead man was being carried out, the only son of his mother, and she was a widow; and a sizeable crowd from the city was with her.* —Luke 7:11–12

The Church of the Widow's Son in Nein, a structure built by the Franciscans in the late nineteenth century over the foundations of a church from the Byzantine period. The modern city of Nazareth is visible on top of the ridge in the distance, left.

Jesus was moved by what he saw. Stopping, touching, and then speaking to the body of the woman's only son, Jesus brought the lad back to life. The response from the crowd was ecstatic:

"A great prophet has risen among us!" and,
"God has visited His people!" —Luke 7:16

A great prophet has arisen—again! God visits his people—again! In our hour of greatest need, God stops, then bends down to touch us, speak to us, and give us life. That he does so is nothing short of miraculous. And to the extent that he empowers us, we too can follow Jesus, going about doing good.

28. "But Why Can't He Be More like Me?"

A drive through Nazareth is an adventure in narrow streets and heavy traffic, punctuated by friendly people at every turn. Today Nazareth is the largest city in the Galilee interior, bustling, busy—and a far cry from the village of Jesus' day. The ancient town owned the tag: "Can any good thing come out of Nazareth?" (John 1:46), and from what we know of the place in the first century AD, that sentiment seems to have been well earned. Unlike today's city,

The Nazareth basin, viewed from the north. The large white building with the conical gray dome is the Basilica of the Annunciation, marking the appearance of the angel to Mary.

all of our data points to the Nazareth of the Gospels being not much of a place.

Geographically, ancient Nazareth sat in a depression atop a high ridge that drops abruptly into the Jezreel Valley to the south. Northward, the ridge falls decisively, though more gently, into the Beth-netopha Valley, the pleasant interior of Galilee. As a result, Nazareth was well off the main lines of traffic that penetrated Galilee in the time of the New Testament. The water and soil resources in the high Nazareth depression were adequate to support a small agricultural village, but certainly didn't attract the attention of folk living in the broad, fertile, and much better connected parts of Galilee. It wasn't a place to draw outside interest or investment, nor one where a resident could ever expect to get rich or be noticed.

The archaeological evidence tells us that first-century Nazareth was a small village of not more than a few dozen families who lived in humble village housing and worked terraced slopes for agriculture. The town covered only a small area on a low rise that today is dominated by the Basilica of the Annunciation and adjacent buildings, circled by tombs; the village springs lay a short walk beyond. There is no archaeological evidence of substantive buildings of any kind—no palaces, administrative centers, marketplaces, or even a synagogue—nor evidence that a village existed on the site in the centuries immediately prior to the first century BC.

And what do we know from ancient texts? Nazareth appears in the Gospels, yes, but not in the writings of Josephus (who knew the region very well) or in any other text from the time of the New Testament, either Jewish, Greek, or Roman. Other than its mention by early church fathers, the name Nazareth appears only in a list of towns and cities where priests lived after the destruction of the temple in AD 70, carved on a marble slab found in Caesarea and dating to the third or fourth century AD.

Mary and Joseph with the lad Jesus, who grew in wisdom and stature in Nazareth. The statue is in the courtyard of the Sisters of Nazareth Convent, Nazareth.

The combined evidence is significant for its insignificance—by every indication, the Nazareth of Jesus' day was off the map of mainstream political, economic, and social life in Galilee.

So who would want to live there? With the help of Josephus's comments on Galilee as a whole, as well as archaeological and geographical data, we can posit that Nazareth was a kind of settlement town where observant Jews whose heart loyalties belonged to Torah and temple came during or just after the time of the Maccabees, in the first century BC, to reestablish or bolster a Jewish

The view from Mount Precipice overlooking the Jezreel Valley, where local memory holds that Jesus jumped in order to flee townsfolk who sought to throw him off the edge. In Hebrew and Arabic, this is "Jumping Mountain."

presence in a Galilee that otherwise was being overrun by the cultural, economic, and religious priorities of Hellenism and then Rome. For both Jews and gentiles, much of Galilee was a very attractive place to live, and many did quite well there. Cana, for instance, was a prosperous Jewish town, the home of can-anything-good-come-out-of-*your*-town Nathaniel (John 21:2). Climbing out of their tight basin, the villagers of Nazareth looked down on a world that in many ways was very successful, and many of its residents likely concluded that that success was tainted by the stain of accommodating the ever-peering eye of a foreign occupying power. Perhaps the best descriptor for Nazareth is that it was provincial, and its residents partisans. It was the kind of a place where mes-

siah talk would have been welcome, as long as the messiah was someone whose priority was to throw off the foreign yoke and return the kingdom to Jerusalem.

Quite early in his public ministry, after spending some time in Capernaum, Jesus returned to Nazareth and spoke in the synagogue (archaeologists haven't found the building; it might have been just a designated room in a house). He read from the prophet Isaiah:

> *"The Spirit of the LORD is upon Me, because He anointed Me to preach the Gospel to the poor. He has sent Me to proclaim release to the captives, and recovery of sight to the blind, to set free those who are oppressed, to proclaim the favorable year of the LORD."*

—Luke 4:18–19; see also Isaiah 61:1–2

If we listen carefully, can we hear Jesus emphasize the word "Me"? Jesus' fellow villagers received the pronouncement eagerly at first, apparently anxious to restore "the kingdom to Israel" (see Acts 1:6), and from their dutiful village of all places. But then the shock. Jesus reminded his townsfolk that Elijah and Elisha, two of the greatest prophets of old, saved . . . gentiles, and not just any gentiles, but a woman of the same ethnicity as Jezebel, and the captain of a Syrian army whose job was to destroy Israel (Luke 4:25–27). Their reaction was rather harsh—the fellows Jesus grew up with tried to toss him off a cliff. From this example, it seems like ancient Nazareth might have been the kind of place that fostered self-focus, tight conformity, and judgment, like a dog barking at its own echo. Perhaps Jesus' in-group extended a bit too far into his compatriots' out-group for comfort. Local tradition identifies the cliff as Mount Precipice, a dramatic drop into the Jezreel Valley on the outskirts of modern Nazareth that provides wonderful vistas to imagine the story.

How do we even begin to define Jesus? Unique? Heroic? Courageous? Innovative? Simple adjectives just don't work. Rabbi? Teacher? Light of the world? Good shepherd? Anointed one? Savior? Yes, certainly, but he is greater than the sum of all these parts. Fully human, fully God. He fulfills all needs, but breaks all molds in doing so. Rather than letting him continue to create me in his image, I tend to make him over in my image. That was what the townsfolk he grew up with in Nazareth tried to do, those who knew him best yet didn't know him at all. And the more I make Jesus over to be like me, the less I am compelled to change who I am.

Identifying *that* problem is the start of many solutions.

29. A Place to Call Home

Born in Bethlehem. Exiled to Egypt. Raised in Nazareth. Baptized in the Jordan. Tempted in the wilderness of Judah. Rejected in Nazareth. Then,

> *[Jesus] came and settled in Capernaum,*
> *which is by the sea.*

—Matthew 4:13

The sea, of course, is the Sea of Galilee. Capernaum, Jesus' adopted home (Matt. 9:1; Mark 2:1), sat halfway along its northern shore. The Gospels don't describe Capernaum directly, although they do mention a few important details about the people living

Contemplating the words of Jesus on the Capernaum shore.

there. Josephus, never at a lack for words, was more effusive about the place:

> *Skirting the lake of Gennesar [the Sea of Galilee] . . . lies a region whose natural properties and beauty are very remarkable. There is not a plant which its fertile soil refused to produce, and its cultivators in fact grow every species; the air is so well-tempered that it suits the most opposite varieties. . . . Besides being favored by its genial air, the country is watered by a highly fertilizing spring, called by the inhabitants Capharnaum [Capernaum].*
>
> —Jewish War 3.516–519

Coming ashore at Capernaum. On the far left is the Pilgrimage Church of St. Peter; to its right are the white limestone remains of the synagogue dating to the late Roman period, while on the far right is the red-domed Greek Orthodox church.

Why did Jesus relocate to Capernaum? According to Matthew (4:13) it was to fulfill the expectations of the prophet Isaiah, who foresaw a light dawning on the troubled

lands of Zebulun and Naphtali. The towns didn't exist yet in Isaiah's day, but by the time of the New Testament, the village of Nazareth had been established in the old tribal territory of Zebulun, and Capernaum in Naphtali. But is there anything else that would have drawn Jesus there? Perhaps the people of Capernaum were more receptive to his message than his Nazareth compatriots were (Luke 4:16–31), but Jesus' later condemnation of Capernaum makes us wonder how welcomed he actually was there as well (Matt. 11:21–23). Josephus made Capernaum out to be a rather pleasant place, where someone might want to spend a holiday. His testimony, when combined with evidence from geography, archaeology, and the gospel record, presents a much fuller and more attractive picture of the place that Jesus came to call home than we might otherwise suspect.

To better imagine the Capernaum of Jesus' day, let's ask the question, "If you were a first-century Capernaumite, what would keep you busy all day?" The answers are many. Your livelihood might have been fishing, of course, on the evidence that Capernaum hugs the seashore and that several of Jesus' disciples were fishermen. But there are other indications as well. Capernaum sits exactly halfway between the delta of the Jordan River to the east and some warm springs to the west. The river dumps a continuous supply of rich organic material into the lake (ready-made fish food), while the springs moderate the water temperature so that the fish tend to congregate in the area during the winter. Also, we know from archaeology that Capernaum had more boat docks during the time of the Gospels than any other city on the lake. From this we can assume that other tasks related to fishing happened at Capernaum as well: boat building perhaps, or at least repair; net mending; the curing and preservation of fish; sales and service. Jesus, we recall, was a "carpenter" by trade (Gk. *tekton*; Matt. 13:55; Mark 6:3), a skilled craftsman in local building materials. Should we assume that he laid down the tools of his trade when he moved to Capernaum, or rather that he found productive work in town as rabbis in the first century tended to do (Acts 18:2–3; Mishnah, *Pirke Avoth* 2.2)? Was Jesus curious about how things were built by the folks living in Capernaum? Nobody was building boats back in Nazareth. *Tekton*-ing would have opened a number of ministry doors for him, all of them useful.

Capernaum was also on a major trade route. We know this on the simple principle that main cities were connected by main routes, and Capernaum lay on the shortest route between Tiberias and Bethsaida, the two major cities on the Jewish side of the lake in the first century. We should note that Capernaum was the last town in Galilee as travelers headed east, and the doorway into Galilee for those coming the other direction. From Roman records, we know that Galileans were subject to customs duties when crossing borders, and of course Capernaum had a tax man. We also know from Latin sources that Rome collected taxes from fisherman

who fished inland waters, and so Matthew (Matt. 9:9), stationed at a border town that also had the most fishing docks on the lake, must have been a pretty busy guy. He likely would have known everyone in town personally, for better or worse.

Luke tells us that there was a centurion in Capernaum (Luke 7:2), which means that the town also must have garrisoned 100 Roman soldiers. Most of them probably spent their time monitoring affairs in the region or along the border. Their official duties would have included protecting Matthew's position (and his person) to ensure that Rome reaped its due share of taxes collected (or extorted) from the locals or those passing through. Whatever else people might have done for a living in Capernaum, a visible percentage of them worked for Rome.

Remains of rooms and courtyards belonging to an *insula*, a housing unit common to villages around the Sea of Galilee in the first century. Behind is the Pilgrimage Church of St. Peter, built over the remains of a church from the Byzantine period that was itself built over an *insula* thought to be the home of Peter.

Capernaum, typical of Jewish villages in Galilee, had a synagogue, and some of the town's residents were professionals attached to it. These are the scribes, Pharisees, and Jewish elders with whom Jesus had constant, and often uneasy, contact (Mark 1:21–22; 2:18–19, 24; 3:1–6).

Some of Capernaum's residents certainly were farmers, shepherds, or shopkeepers; others likely worked in cottage industries such as baking bread or making pottery; this would have been typical of any village. But in the ruins of Capernaum archaeologists also found a disproportionately large number of high-quality basalt millstones, enough to suggest that they were not only used in town but manufactured there as well (the local stone is basalt). This made Caper-

A fishing net typical of those used by Jesus' disciples.

naum a center of heavy industry and trade. And let's not forget Josephus. He mentioned that when he broke his arm falling from a horse over in the delta of the Jordan River, he came to Capernaum to see a doctor (*The Life*, 72).

So we see that there was a lot to do in Capernaum, a lot of people coming and going, and a lot for Jesus to do, too. Capernaum was a happenin' place, and Jesus had a lot to offer. His skills were practical, personal, and *useful*. And by watching him, we can get a sense of how to be the same wherever we live.

30. Inscribed in Stone

History has rarely been kind to women. Ancient texts of all kinds, including those from the Middle East, generally ignore their deeds, or tend to portray women as unprotected, helpless, or connivers in what was otherwise a man's world (Deborah, Jael, and Elizabeth are vigorous exceptions). When a woman does appear in a story—even a biblical one—she is often not named. It's Manoah and the wife of Manoah, Elijah and the widow of Zarephath, or Simon and the mother-in-law of Simon, for instance (Judg. 13:3; 1 Kings 17:9; Mark 1:30). We can debate whether the biblical writers were reflecting the culture of the day or setting it; still, it sure would be nice if we knew these women's names.

Among Jesus' many followers were twelve men whom he chose as apostles: Simon Peter, Andrew, James and John, Philip, Bartholomew, Matthew, Thomas, James son of Alphaeus, Simon the Zealot, Thaddaeus (or Judas son of James), and Judas Iscariot (Matt. 10:2–4; Mark 3:16–19; Luke 6:13–16). Often the gospel writers called them disciples; we might also say pupils of the master, or apprentices. Certainly they were followers of Jesus; over time they also became believers. We take it for granted that they were all men. What we mustn't forget is that Jesus also had many followers who were women. Luke supplies what must be only a partial list:

Soon afterwards, [Jesus] began going around from one city and village to another, proclaiming and preaching the kingdom of God. The twelve were with Him, and also some women who had been healed of evil spirits and sicknesses: Mary who was called Magdalene, from whom seven demons had gone out, and Joanna the wife of Chuza, Herod's steward, and Susanna, and many others who were contributing to their support out of their private means.

—Luke 8:1–3

We tend to emphasize these women's "pasts," as if the twelve guys were chosen because they were all Mr. Right. Mary Magdalene especially has fared badly in commentary and modern tabloid fare. An unnamed prostitute appears in the story prior (Luke 7:36–50), and many Bible readers connect her with Mary Magdalene, although others (myself included) see little historical

The synagogue at Magdala, dating to the time of the New Testament. It is likely that Jesus attended Sabbath services with the residents of Magdala here.

The altar of the *Duc in Altum* church, Magdala.

or literary support for doing so. We know that Mary Magdalene was with Jesus all the way to the cross and the empty tomb, something his male disciples had trouble doing (John 19:25; 20:1). But can we know more?

Recent archaeological excavations at Magdala can suggest a context. Magdala is a newly excavated site on the northwestern shore of the Sea of Galilee, midway between Jesus' home base at Capernaum and Tiberias, the capital of Galilee. The town commanded the southern end of the Plain of Gennesaret (Matt. 14:34), the breadbasket of Tiberias, and so profited both from resources and trade. Magdala is not mentioned in the Bible other than in Mary's label Magdalene, "of Magdala," but a town called Magadan, likely the same place, is (Matt. 15:39). Mark 8:10 gives an alternate name, Dalmanutha, for what appears to be the same location. The Aramaic name was Midgal Nunya, "Fish Tower." The historian Josephus and the geographer Strabo, both writing in the first century, mention a prominent town called Tarichaeae, "Salted Fish," in the same area (*Jewish War* 2.596–609; *Geography* 16.2.45). This gives us a fifth name for the place, or at least evidence of a very crowded portion of the seashore.

Excavations at Magdala have uncovered surprising finds, all dating to the time of the New Testament: a seawall, harbor and docks, holding tanks and places to process fish, shops, residential areas, and right-angled streets. Archaeologists also found *miqve'ot,* ritual immersion baths, at Magdala that were filled by high groundwater, and a synagogue. Everything was built with the highest quality of workmanship. The synagogue is especially noteworthy: its floors were of mosaic, its walls covered with the same frescoed designs as the palaces of the Herodian family, and in the center was a large block of limestone intricately carved with Jewish symbols, including a menorah. This stone block may have been the chair of the local rabbi (the "chair of Moses"; see Matt. 23:2), or a table on which to enthrone the Torah scroll. Clearly the Jewish community in Magdala was both prosperous and observant, so its most famous resident, Mary Magdalene, may have also been successful in whatever her occupation and situation in life was. And she not only followed Jesus but sacrificed personally (Luke 8:2–3) so that his ministry could proceed unhindered.

The site of ancient Magdala is owned by the Legionaries of Christ, a Roman Catholic congregation of priests who focus on Christlike spirituality. On a portion of the site they have erected a church consecrated as *Duc in Altum*, "Put Out into the Deep Water" (Luke 5:4). Its altar is in the form of a boat, the boat's mast is in the form of a cross, and the open sea is visible through the eastern glass wall. Upon entering the church, visitors pass through the Women's Atrium, a large round hall with eight circumference pillars. Inscribed in stone on seven are the names of women whom the Gospels say followed Jesus: Mary Magdalene (Luke 8:2), Susanna and Joanna (Luke 8:3), Mary and Martha (Luke 10:38–39), Salome the mother of James and John (Mark 15:40; and Matt. 20:20 in early tradition), the mother-in-law of Simon Peter (Matt. 8:14–15), Mary wife of Clopas (John 19:25), and the "many other women" of Mark 15:41. The eighth pillar is unmarked, intended for female disciples of Jesus throughout history. But let's make it personal. When I take students into the Women's Atrium at Magdala, I ask the women in the group to look at the unmarked pillar, and I say, "That one's yours. Your name is inscribed there." This pillar is for every woman like Mary Magdalene, who seeks to follow Jesus through the cross to the empty tomb.

The Mary Magdalene pillar in the Women's Atrium of the *Duc in Altum* church.

31. "For the Wind Was Contrary"

Signposts: Galilee, Sea of Galilee

The Sea of Galilee stands front and center as the arena of much of Jesus' public ministry (Matt. 4:18; 15:29; Mark 1:16; 7:31). Yet for all of its singularity in the travels of Jesus it is almost never mentioned in the Old Testament. When it is, it appears more often in descriptions of tribal borders (Num. 34:11; Josh. 12:3; 13:27) than in stories (Josh. 11:2). That's a bit odd, given that it is the only permanent natural freshwater lake for 500 miles and as such must have been an active center of living, fishing, and trading for millennia. On the other hand, the sea is prominent in the works of

Heavy clouds pass over the Sea of Galilee in early evening; clear skies to the west forecast clear sailing tonight. It wasn't always so.

the first-century historian Josephus, who typically called it "the lake of Gennesar" (*Jewish War* 3.506); Israelis today simply say "the Kinneret." Josephus was a native Galilean proud of his roots and didn't spare flowery adjectives: the sea was "sweet to the taste . . . excellent to drink . . . clearer than marsh water [I'm not sure how much of a compliment that one is] . . . perfectly pure . . . has an agreeable temperature" and so on (*Jewish War* 3.506–507). Mark Twain, singularly unimpressed with its bare perimeter when he visited the region in 1867, went overboard in the other direction, severely downgrading the sea in comparison to the natural beauty of Lake Tahoe (*The Innocents Abroad*, chapter 48). I guess the truth must lie somewhere in between.

Evening on the Sea of Galilee. The waves are agitated.

Like all bodies of water, the Sea of Galilee records the moods of the weather. Its color changes with the cloud cover and humidity;

its temperature with the seasons; its surface with the wind. Most of the year air temperatures are moderate to hot, the weather calm and the humidity high, making the sea a working lake for fishing and transportation. As was typical throughout history, the villages around the lake in the time of the New Testament shared its resources and moods. We don't have stories that mention how wonderful it was to sail the sea's perimeter or cross its width in good weather; still, Jesus' fishermen disciples must have loved their connection to the fresh, open vista of the waters on which they plied their trade.

What we do have are stories of storms. Local fishermen today report that the highest waves they have experienced reach nearly six feet. Even with all the safety equipment mandated for modern watercraft, they stay off the sea in rough weather. The disciples weren't so fortunate.

The Sea of Galilee is ringed by hills rising as much as 1,300 feet from its surface. These give the people living along the shore a bit of a hemmed-in, protected feel. But they also have consequences for sailing. For one, the hills block a distant horizon-line view of incoming clouds—and hence wind and rain—that may be approaching from over the Mediterranean. First-century seafarers had some rudimentary skills in weather forecasting based on the color of the sky (Matt. 16:2–3), but without a distant view from the surface of the Sea of Galilee, anticipating changes in the weather was an especially unpredictable endeavor. What was predictable is the pattern of cool winds that blow off the Mediterranean in the morning, pick up by midday as the warmed Galilean air rises, and typically reach the Sea of Galilee by mid- or late afternoon. The force of these prevailing westerly winds is increased by the terrain over which they blow. The hills of lower Galilee run as west-east ridges, with wide valleys between that channel the winds directly to the Sea of Galilee. If the winds are strong, and especially if they are fueled by Mediterranean storms, they sweep down the steep rise along the Sea of Galilee's western shore and churn its water into an angry mass. When we remember that the boats of the first century sat rather low in the water and that most ancient Galileans had a distrust, or even fear, of the sea anyway (see Ps. 107:23–32; Isa. 57:20), we have a perfect recipe for a dangerous voyage.

The Gospels speak of two times when Jesus and his disciples were caught in a storm at night on the open sea (Matt. 14:22–33; Mark 4:35–41; 6:47–52; Luke 8:22–25). In one, Jesus had fallen asleep in the stern of the boat as waves broke over the side; awakened, he stilled the surging water with "Hush, be still," words that otherwise may silence a squalling baby—or a band of detractors (Mark 4:39; see also Ps. 107:29). In the other, Jesus walked to his terrified disciples amid the churning waves:

> *The boat was already a long distance from the land, battered by the waves; for the wind was contrary. And in the fourth watch of the night He came to them,*

walking on the sea. When the disciples saw Him walking on the sea, they were terrified, and said, "It is a ghost!" And they cried out in fear. —Matthew 14:24–26

The gospel of Mark adds that the disciples were "straining at the oars, for the wind was against them" (Mark 6:48). They recognized Jesus only when he calmed the sea (Matt. 14:28, 32–33).

What would they have thought if he had decided to just ride out the storm with them instead, as he often does during storms in our own lives?

Surging waters. Choppy seas. Dark horizons. Forces far beyond our control. We struggle with every bit of energy and wit that we have, without orientation as to where we are or how to get where we should be.

And too often, like those early disciples, we tend to think that Jesus is worth following only if he gets us out of our troubles first.

The preserved remains of the hull a boat that sailed the Sea of Galilee in the first century. Called the Ancient Galilee Boat by Israelis and the Jesus Boat by Christian tourists, this boat was typical of those used by Jesus and his disciples. It is on display in the Yigal Alon Center at Kibbutz Ginosar on the northwestern side of the Sea of Galilee.

Signposts:
Galilee, Sea of
Galilee, Hippos,
Capernaum

32. The City on a Hill

Every once in a while, a new student will say to me, "I wish I had been told that some sites were ruined and not as they would have been during Bible times." Or, "I thought that when I came to the Holy Land, somehow it would look more ancient than it does." I guess that's fair, but the Holy Land gallops forward just like everywhere else: styles of dress, modes of transport and communication, forms of architecture, how to live off the land—all aspects of material culture in the lands of the Bible have changed over time, and sometimes even improved. Even the local terrain, most of it hard limestone, takes on new forms here and there,

The Decapolis city Hippos was located on this flat-topped hill, a prominent landmark on the eastern shore of the Sea of Galilee, above the kibbutz En Gev.

shaped by construction equipment and jack-hammers. But what hasn't changed is the overall geographical shape of the land, the horizon line on which life is lived.

When we stand on the Capernaum shore and look out over the Sea of Galilee, scanning the waterline as it sweeps away left and right, then meets again at the far southern shore, or when we run our eyes across the hilly horizon line above, we are allowed to erase from our vision the electric lights, the asphalt roads, the large blocky buildings, the groves of banana plants covered with hothouse polycarbonate sheeting, and imagine. Imagine Jesus' view, or the view of his disciples, evening after evening as the sun set behind the same row of hills that it does today, under the same blue then orangey sky. From archaeology we know where the towns and cities around the lake were in the time of the New Testament, and where the small fishing boats put to shore. And we can hear the same lap of the waves, or voices calling over the water.

Matthew's gospel gives prominence to the Sermon on the Mount. There's no way of knowing which mount this was, although faithful claimants abound. Likely it was somewhere on the sea's northern shore. The language of Jesus' discourse is both specific and eternal, pithy and to the point, yet prompts us as readers to unpack from it applications for our own lives. Here and there in the sermon Jesus spoke in short parables:

"You are the light of the world. A city set on a hill cannot be hidden; nor does anyone light a lamp and put it under a basket, but on the lampstand, and it gives light to all who are in the house. Let your light shine before men in such a way that they may see your good works, and glorify your Father who is in heaven." —Matthew 5:14–16

Here we have a parable embedded within a parable, the metaphor of a city on a hill placed between metaphors of light. Jesus often spoke of light as a metaphor for truth, for right behavior, or for divine revelation (John 8:12; 9:5; 12:36). But this is the only time he mentioned a city on a hill. The combination of images prompts us to picture a city at dusk or nightfall, as lamps are lit and before the working fires of the day are dampened down, yet when light can already be discerned at a considerable distance.

Theologians are fond of understanding this city on a hill as Jerusalem, either the city at the time of the New Testament or the New Jerusalem of the age to come. It's a bit of an odd suggestion, given that historic Jerusalem was actually hidden among the hills and completely out of sight until a traveler came right upon it (see Pss. 121:1; 125:2). Nor should we necessarily think that the crowds hearing Jesus' words were thinking of the prophecy of Isaiah: "in the last days the mountain of the house of the LORD . . . will be raised above the hills" (Isa. 2:2). Equally creative was John Winthrop, the first governor of the Massachusetts colony, who in 1630 described his New World community

"as a city upon a hill; the eyes of all people are upon us." Particularized to the American national endeavor, the phrase has become a beacon of light for presidents and political aspirants from John Kennedy on.

But as a parable, the city on a hill must make sense first within the real-life, visible context of its original hearers. That is, like all parables, it must point first to the cultural and geographical horizon of those who actually heard Jesus' words. Since people in Jesus' time usually didn't travel widely and were often illiterate (or nearly so), we should recognize that the context is foremost Galilee, and perhaps most immediately the northern end of the sea, even if the Sermon on the Mount contains sayings that Jesus would have repeated to many audiences in many places.

Although most of the archaeological remains of Hippos date to the centuries following the New Testament, they represent a cultural trajectory toward Greco-Roman paganism that was already present in the land during the time of the New Testament. This row of columns in the city forum fell, like dominos, in the earthquake of AD 749.

The only city on a hill visible from Capernaum, or from the hillside above, was Hippos, just off the eastern side of the Sea of Galilee. And what a city it was! Hippos was not just a prominent urban area but a Greek city, a *polis*, one of the Decapolis cities (see Mark 5:20; 7:31) that were founded south and east of the sea with the express purpose of disseminating Hellenistic, pagan culture in the region. The Decapolis cities fostered cultural and religious values that were diametrically opposed to those of "the lost sheep of the house of Israel" (Matt. 10:6). While the magnificent archaeological remains on the site date to the centuries following the New Testament, they neverthe-

Corinthian capitals carved from basalt, the local bedrock at Hippos, once decorated the late Roman city. They represent the enduring beauty and power of Rome.

less portray the attractive choice that pulled Galileans toward Rome in Jesus' day. Jesus recognized the cultural clash that lay at his door and was seducing his people away from the lifestyle standards embodied in the call of God. So he addressed it up front, using the real language of every day. To paraphrase: "That city on a hill. They're shining *their* light. They're spreading *their* understanding of what makes for right behavior and truth. Now you need to do the same, so that by seeing *your* good deeds, people will give glory to the Father in heaven."

33. A Splash of Color

Among the toys scattered around the house when I was a child it seems as though there was always a cardboard kaleidoscope lying around somewhere, tucked in the back of a drawer or squeezed under a couch cushion. I remember holding the round tube up to the window, looking into the small eyepiece and twisting the end. With every twist was a splash of color as bits of transparent cellophane or plastic fell into new patterns, each, like the proverbial snowflake, different from the one before. Since our TV was black and white, this was real entertainment. Of course once in a while the colors fell into an unattractive blob, but I only had to twist the end again and hope for better next time.

I haven't had the pleasure of looking into a kaleidoscope for many years. Now that I live in Israel, I'm sometimes reminded that the mix of people who live here is something like a kaleidoscope—countless folk from all over the world, as well as many whose families have lived in the land for centuries, each with a unique combination of social, cultural, and religious qualities and each, at any given time or place, rubbing shoulders with others, equally unique in their own right. Splashes of color forming patterns, and then, down the street or over the next hill, similar folk forming different patterns with others, sometimes in surprising and pleasant ways, but unfortunately all too often overlapping in a much less attractive manner.

When my children were in elementary and middle school they attended a camp in Israel sponsored by a Baptist denomination. For several years the camp was held on the grounds of a kibbutz (an Israeli collective farming community) just south of the Sea of Galilee. One year, my son Ben invited Yousef, a school friend from a Muslim family, to camp. So there we have it—a Muslim attending a Christian camp on a Jewish kibbutz. A splash of color. Unexpected? Here, not really, but certainly pleasant in any case.

Orthodox Jews at the Western Wall, Jerusalem.

When my wife, Diane, dropped Ben and Yousef off at the camp, she started chatting with Itzik, a fellow who happened to be on the kibbutz that day. He was from Haifa, a large Israeli city on the Mediterranean coast, a place without any specific biblical attachment to the past. And so Itzik, in his native Israeli Hebrew accent, commented, "I like living in Haifa. It's a place where Moses wasn't, Jesus wasn't, and Muhammad wasn't. People get along there."

Ouch.

Armenian priests remembering Jesus' body, anointed for burial, at the XIII Station of the Cross in the Church of the Holy Sepulchre.

The fact that Haifa has seen its share of bus bombings is irrelevant. For Itzik—and for many others living in Israel today—the colors of the kaleidoscope fall into an ugly mass only when religion gets involved. Take out Moses, take out Jesus, and take out Muhammad, together with the deeply exclusive feelings that the Jews, Christians, and Muslims have for their own understanding of God and his will for this world, and life will be the way it's supposed to be—bright splashes of harmonious, beautiful color. In

our secular, humanistic world, God's will, together with the outward expression of that will by the actions of his followers, is usually seen to be part of the problem, not part of the solution.

Appropriately, my pastor in Jerusalem once commented, "This land is full of people with religious hearts, but not loving hearts." I dare say that I agree, but hasten to add that this is not a problem unique to the Holy Land. Indeed, the words of the apostle Paul strike home wherever we live:

An observant Muslim, barefoot, prays toward Mecca in the open desert without the aid of a mosque.

> *[I pray] . . . that He would grant you, according to the riches of His glory, to be strengthened with power through His Spirit in the inner man, so that Christ may dwell in your hearts through faith; and that you, being rooted and grounded in love, may be*

able to comprehend with all the saints what is the breadth and length and height and depth, and to know the love of Christ which surpasses knowledge, that you may be filled up to all the fullness of God. —Ephesians 3:16–19

There's something here that is deeper than mere human expressions of religion. The love of Christ, the Messiah, working miracles of color in our lives, surpasses knowledge— even our feeble knowledge of what it means to be religious. While God desires that all of us acknowledge his grace with a response that is heartfelt and biblically based, he wants most of all that we know and experience his love as it is revealed in Jesus. How else can unattractive blobs display the brilliance for which they were created?

34. Ozymandius, Hazor-Style

Percy Bysshe Shelley's 1818 poem "Ozymandias" captures the lost grandeur of once-proud pharaonic Egypt. The title is a Greek form of one of the throne names of Rameses II, arguably the greatest of pharaohs. During his sixty-seven-year reign, Rameses II erected massive monuments in stone to his gods and to himself. Many can still be seen in broken form, preserving their splendor yet today. The largest, a statue of Rameses II, once stood over six stories tall; its "shattered visage" is likely the inspiration for the poem. Rameses was a great warrior, a tremendous builder, and a prodigious father; he bore over 100 children in an attempt to ensure his legacy. But Shelley's

This toppled statue of Rameses II once dominated the Ramasseum Temple on the west bank of the Nile, opposite Luxor, Egypt. The Ramasseum was dedicated to the exploits of Rameses II.

poem, written in the swell tide of British and French efforts at empire building, ends with the candid lines:

"My name is Ozymandias, King of Kings,
Look on my Works, ye Mighty, and despair!"
Nothing beside remains. Round the decay
Of that colossal Wreck, boundless and bare
The lone and level sands stretch far away.

"Ozymandius" has become Shelley's best-known work, a template for human greatness and its inevitable decay. In the world of the Bible, perhaps the best parallel is the Canaanite city of Hazor.

Every bit of data that we can derive from archaeology, from ancient texts, and from Hazor's geographical setting combines to verify the claim that in the centuries prior

The pillared remains of an Israelite warehouse at Hazor overlook a stubbled field that covers the once-powerful Canaanite city.

to Israel's entrance into the land, this was the most important of the Canaanite cities, well deserving the sobriquet "the head of all these kingdoms" (Josh. 11:10). As its excavator Amnon Ben-Tor is wont to say, "There is Hazor, and there is every place else."

Hazor was a major stop on the great trunk route of antiquity that linked Mesopotamia with Egypt, supplying the route with tin, textiles, precious metals, and luxury goods, and reaping economic benefits that befit the city's cosmopolitan character in return. But what made its geographical position unique is that Hazor commanded the southern end of the Huleh Valley, a narrow basin lying between Mount Hermon and the Sea of Galilee that channeled most of the international traffic flowing through Canaan on its way. Hazor plugged the bottom of this funnel. No one could get by without encountering the place, and everyone benefited from the economic and cultural forces that flowed through. And the political climate in Mesopotamia and Egypt, the productive superpowers commanding both ends of this route, was brisk enough throughout the middle and late Bronze Ages that Hazor prospered immensely.

It was during this time—essentially the period between Abraham and Joshua—that Hazor reached its zenith in size, wealth, and world influence. The mound that remains measures 200 acres, by far the largest footprint of any ancient city in Canaan and one that rivaled other great cities of the day such as Ur and Babylon. The archaeological finds reveal a city that was cosmopolitan, elegant, imposing—and literate, at least according to the standard of the day. Cuneiform texts found at Hazor, written in a wedge-script on clay, include legal documents, lexical lists, letters, divination texts, a mathematical table, and administrative economic documents. Together these show that Hazor was connected to trading interests throughout the then-known world. By every indication, thousands of undiscovered texts remain hidden in the mound, waiting to be excavated. When they are found—and this will be a matter of time, effort, and (I hate to say it) luck—the archive of Hazor will hopefully enrich our understanding of the world into which Israel entered to settle and live more than any other discovery in the land so far.

Excavations show that Hazor was violently destroyed by fire in the middle of the thirteenth century BC, a date that nicely corresponds to Joshua's destruction of the city (see Josh. 11:13, "Israel did not burn any cities that stood on their mounds, except Hazor alone, which Joshua burned"). Israel rebuilt Hazor in the centuries following (see 1 Kings 9:15), but on a much smaller scale, only one-twentieth the size. And, in the inevitable cycle of urban growth and decline, it too was violently destroyed, this time by the Assyrians in the days of Isaiah the prophet. Hazor functioned for Israel the same way that it had functioned all along—as the key gateway guarding the all-important northern approaches into the land. Its destruction in the late eighth century BC sent shockwaves of impending doom throughout Israel and

Judah, opening the way for the obliteration of the Northern Kingdom a decade later and nearly devastating the Southern Kingdom twenty years after that.

Isaiah, a man of keen vision and tremendous communicative skill, was active as a prophet in Jerusalem when the Assyrians blew through. He had something to say:

> *He it is who reduces rulers to nothing, who makes the judges of the earth meaningless. Scarcely have they been planted, scarcely have they been sown, scarcely has their stock taken root in the earth, but He merely blows on them, and they wither, and the storm carries them away like stubble.*
>
> —Isaiah 40:23–24

Reconstructed remains of the Israelite watchtower at Hazor, built to warn its inhabitants of the oncoming Assyrian attack in the late eighth century BC.

Isaiah's metaphor jumps to life when we gaze at the crop of wheat that local farmers sow across the vast stretch of fertile soil covering most of the long-buried city today. Green and tender in late winter, its stubble is seared by the winds that scour the mound in the blast furnace of summer. Scarcely here, then gone—it's a pattern of life, in our time as much as Isaiah's.

It's time to take stock.

- ✣ Life is transient in the best of situations. Check.

- ✣ The forces that work to destroy our efforts, our worldviews, and our physical and moral comforts are unyielding. Check.

- ✣ Most of these we can't control anyway. Check.

So what lasts?

> *All flesh is grass, and all its loveliness is like the flower of the field. The grass withers, the flower fades, when the breath of the* LORD *blows upon it; surely the people are grass. The grass withers, the flower fades, but the word of our God stands forever.*

> —Isaiah 40:6–8

Double-check.

35. "But I'm Only Human!"

Soaring to a height of over 9,200 feet, Mount Hermon dominates the northern landscape of Israel. The mountain is actually the southern end of a long north-south range separating Syria from Lebanon; Damascus nestles beneath its eastern slope, while to the west lies the Beqa'a Valley in the rugged Lebanese interior. Only the southern tip of the Hermon range is in Israel, standing like a solitary sentinel over Galilee. From its peak, it's possible with high-powered binoculars to see the skyscrapers of Tel Aviv 100 miles to the south, or read the numbers on the license plates of vehicles in Damascus.

Mount Hermon in January. One of the mountain's Arabic nicknames is Jebel es-Sheikh, "Old Man Mountain," labeling its white pate.

For the ancient Israelites, Mount Hermon was one of the greatest symbols of the on-going blessing of God, blessings that the biblical writers often likened to a well-watered, fertile land. Heavy snows cover Mount Hermon every winter, and their slow melt fills the huge aquifers within the mountain's limestone core. Then, every second of every hour throughout the year, an average of 5,000 gallons of clear, cold water gush from Hermon's springs into Israel's marshy Huleh Valley, out of which flows the Jordan River. In a dry and thirsty land, the region of Mount Hermon is always green, always fertile, always blessed.

But for the writers of the Old Testament, Mount Hermon also symbolized the loca-

The spring at Dan, the largest in the Middle East and the primary source of the Jordan River.

tion of the natural northern boundary of Israel. Beyond Hermon's massive bulk lay the rightful homeland of the Gentiles— Phoenicians in Lebanon and Arameans in Damascus and beyond. Hermon's foreboding height reflected Israel's attitude toward its northern neighbors, where foreign relations were—and still are—characterized by mutual caution, suspicion, and dread.

Throughout the period of the Old Testament, the Israelite city of Dan, lying off Hermon's southwestern slope, guarded the largest of the springs of the Jordan River. This was a city blessed by an overabundance of water, yet one that sat under the constant shadow of foreign domination. Moreover, it was here that Jeroboam had erected a cult site to rival the temple in Jerusalem, thereby combining worship of the Lord with that of the indigenous Canaanite and Phoenician fertility deities, Baal and Asherah (1 Kings 12:29–33). By embracing these "sins of Jeroboam" (2 Kings 17:21–23), the Israelites attempted to play both sides of the loyalty fence. Over time, Israel's original goal of fostering a distinctive lifestyle based on the unique character of God was blurred beyond recognition.

By the late seventh century BC, after the northern kingdom of Israel had fallen, these fatal patterns of social and religious behavior had also become hopelessly ingrained in Judah. In response, the prophet Jeremiah cut to the core, calling on the surrounding nations to sit in judgment on God's people:

Therefore thus says the LORD, *"Ask now among the nations, who ever heard the like of this? The virgin of Israel has done a most appalling thing."*

—Jeremiah 18:13

What terrible thing had Israel done? To illustrate his answer, Jeremiah first asked two rhetorical questions:

"Does the snow of Lebanon forsake the rock of the open country? Or is the cold flowing water from a foreign land ever snatched away?"

—Jeremiah 18:14

Knowing well the characteristics of Mount Hermon, Jeremiah's audience no doubt answered with a resounding, "No! There's always snow somewhere on Mount Hermon! Its springs always flow!" (In the higher elevations of Mount Hermon up in Lebanon, snow typically does remain through the summer, even though it nearly always disappears from the southern, Israel-facing slopes.) Then, having secured his people's own admission that the elements of nature always do what they're supposed to, Jeremiah turned the tables on them:

"For My people have forgotten Me, they burn incense to worthless gods and they have stumbled from their ways, from the ancient paths, to walk in bypaths, not on a highway, to make their land a desolation."

—Jeremiah 18:15–16

Mountains, snow, springs—inanimate objects like these do exactly what they were created to do. But *people*—the very creatures who were made in God's image (Gen. 1:27) with minds to commune with him, don't. It's sometimes the lives of the people who at first seem to be the most blessed that end up being the most wasted in the end—dry, empty, and unproductive, like Jeremiah's warning of coming desolation to this once-blessed land. The powerful springs of Mount Hermon flow every day. Shouldn't our attention to the things of God be as unrelenting?

The sacred precinct at Dan, dating to the time of the Israelite monarchy.

36. About-Face!

When it comes to accessing natural resources, not all parts of the land of ancient Israel are created equal. Lacking substantial mineral resources (well, there is a lot of limestone), it's all about available soil and water, with pride of place given to the large inland valleys and coastal plain. When we consider that these flatlands also carried the major through routes of the region, we can easily see why they were more populous, connected, and cosmopolitan than the

hill country and steppe lands bordering the desert to the south and east.

The coastal plain lay just outside of Israel's control for most of the biblical period. For folk living up in the Judean hills, the coast was tempting for all that it offered, but feared for some of the same reasons. Open and exposed, full of opportunity yet vulnerable, the coast was most of all a place of competing—and compelling—worldviews that didn't necessarily line up with those of Moses and the prophets.

Caesarea: Where the land of ancient Israel met the ravenous world of Rome. The protruding shoreline was once the man-made foundation of the deep-sea harbor built by Herod the Great.

Both this object and its material, white marble, are foreign to Israel, yet compellingly beautiful. Though this statue dates to the late Roman period, its substance represents the challenges facing the Jews of Judea in the time of the New Testament.

In the time of the Old Testament, the main line of international traffic ran the length of the coastal plain, parallel to the sea. But with the coming of Greece and then Rome, the route swung around ninety degrees so that the land lanes became sea lanes. With that shift, the cultural, political, and material reality of the Mediterranean world washed into New Testament Judea like waves that just don't stop. Some of the folk up in the hills had been waiting for a chance to reap "the abundance of the seas" that followed (Deut. 33:19; see also Isa. 23:8; Ezek. 27:27); most were either skeptical or fearful of the implications. The Phoenicians, Israel's old-time neighbor to the northwest, were precursors of the threat (Isa. 23; Ezek. 27:1–28:24). The late New Testament scholar Sean Freyne spoke of Israel's "grudging admiration" of these seagoers: Many Israelites wanted to be as successful as they were, but they didn't like their methods in becoming so.

Herod the Great linked the dry-land province of Judea to the heart of the Roman world through a brand-new port city, Caesarea. Its infrastructure surpassed in technological skill nearly everything that was being built elsewhere in the world at that time. While most of the things that visitors to Caesarea see today date to later periods, the city already had everything a proper Roman city should have by the time of the New Testament. These include a harbor, theatre and amphitheatre, palaces (including one jutting into the sea), civic halls and a temple dedicated to Caesar Augustus (the first Caesar to declare himself a god; that's difficult to do!), and a grid street pattern with underground sewers—all built in an architectural style that showed it belonged in Rome, not Judea (*Jewish War* 1.408–415; *Jewish Antiquities* 15.331–341). By building Caesarea, Herod formalized the means by which Rome attempted to establish a new reality in Judea, changing its sacred identity in the process. Caesarea, not Jerusalem, was now the seat of government, of imperial power, of unlimited economic opportunities and of a cultural ambiance that was seductive and compelling. This fact on the ground was especially troubling to the Jewish soul that embraced *shalom*, a Torah-centric life the way it was supposed to be, grounded in a language and set of God-given promises oriented to the Judean heartland.

And then Jesus said:

*"You shall be my witnesses both in
Jerusalem, and in all Judea and Samaria,
and even to the remotest part [the ends] of
the earth."*

—Acts 1:8

Herod the
Great built this
aqueduct to carry
fresh water to
Caesarea. He
would have been
comfortable in
the beach-going
atmosphere it
attracts today, a
far cry from the
conservative air
of Jerusalem.

The book of Acts follows exactly this geo-graphical sequence, from Jerusalem to Samaria to Rome, with perhaps the most significant conceptual move in Acts 9 and 10. It was Peter who took the step from the Judean heartland out to the beginning of the ends of the earth. The same Peter

who knew the other sea, the useful fresh-water one we call the Sea of Galilee. Peter went first to Lydda (modern Lod, adjacent to Ben Gurion Airport today), where the Judean hills drop onto the plain, then straight out to Joppa, where he stayed with a fellow of the same name (Simon), in a city that, while on the shoreline, historically at least had been linked to Judea (Acts 9:32–43). So he entered the coastal plain, but in a manner that wasn't too far out of his comfort zone. Then he received the call to go up the coast to Caesarea (Acts 10:9–23). Peter saw a sheet descending out of heaven (as noted by professor Linford Stutzman, the same Greek term (*othonē*) designates the large, white, square sails of Mediterranean ships), full to the brim with all sorts of strange and ritually unclean and nonkosher things. But God said, "Eat!" And then, "Head on up to Caesarea!" To a city dedicated to the divine Caesar. For an appointment with Cornelius, the centurion in charge of the Italian cohort, sent to enforce the will of Rome (Acts 10:1, 22).

Peter embodied the scrupulously observant reality of an ancient people wrapped in the promises of God. Cornelius represented what the entire known world was on its way to becoming. Several years ago one of my students, an insightful woman by the name of Barbara, asked, "What would happen if the people who see only the past and the people that see only the future were to turn around and face each other?"

Once opened, the barrier of the seashore let in a rising tide. Rome intended Caesarea to be its entry point into Judea; Peter, gulping hard, about-faced the process so that it became the gateway of the gospel to the most remote parts of the earth. It's amazing how far the gospel can spread when those carrying it see not only the needs in the lives of others, but the needs in their own lives as well.

37. There's a Little Jacob in All of Us

The term Transjordan gained favor as a place name for lands lying east of the Jordan River following the First World War, when the Middle East was under European control. As such, the term views those lands from the perspective of the West. The equivalent term in the Old Testament, "beyond the Jordan," was actually used both ways, depending on whether the view across was toward the east (Deut. 3:8; Josh. 12:1) or toward the west (Deut. 3:20; Josh. 12:7).

The Jabbok River, scene of Jacob's encounter with the angel of God. Somewhere in the vicinity Jacob became Israel.

Indeed, lying behind the term is a recognition that the lands separated by the yawning chasm of the Jordan Valley are two halves of a whole. The social and political history of the region, some of which is recorded in the Bible, bears this out.

When we compare the living spaces east and west of the Jordan River, we find the same underlying bedrock on both sides, as well as the same types of soil produced from the rock. Rainfall patterns are also similar—precipitation falls at the same times of year and comes from the same direction,

although the proportion lessens the further east we go. The two sides also have many of the same plants and animals, both domesticated and wild. Not surprisingly, the human inhabitants are similar too: they're shepherds, vine tenders, wheat growers, living in villages and market towns, using the same methods to adapt to the landscape. And the processes by which shepherds settled down to become villagers, and villages became towns and then walled cities and eventually nation-states, pattern out in familiar ways in both regions called "beyond the Jordan." A major international trade route also bisected

The highlands of Gilead, cleft by the Jabbok River. Today, the river is widened into a lake formed by the King Talal Dam.

each, running north-south to connect Asia with Africa and the Arabian Peninsula, linking people living east and west of the Jordan River to the world beyond in the process. All of this is not to say that there aren't differences between the two regions: the primary one is that the lands to the east are bordered by the vast North Arabian Desert, with the continued threat of invasion or famine always lurking at the door. But we must remember that the lands in the west face the open Mediterranean Sea, also a source of invasion and storm. Perhaps the differences are overplayed.

In any case, the connectedness between east and west may be seen best in Gilead, a region of hard limestone hills that rises eastward from the Jordan Valley. Opposite, to the west, is the territory of Ephraim and Manasseh, the hard limestone heartland of the northern kingdom of Israel. The vistas and living conditions are similar in each, giving an ecological kinship to people looking at each other across the rift between. The Gilead highlands are eroded on an east-west line by the mighty cleft of the Jabbok River, which drains its many hills and vales into the Jordan. This cleft was the historic heartland of Gad, the most dominant of the eastern Israelite tribes (Josh. 13:24–28; 22:9). Most of the stories recorded in the Bible that took place east of the Jordan happened within the vicinity of these Gilead hills. Of them, the founding story is Jacob's.

Jacob was as his name implied. The root of the word means "the heel of a foot"; as a verb, "to follow at the heel" or, figuratively, "to grab at the heel and overcome"; hence the adjective "deceitful," sometimes synonymous with "being clever." Jacob made a

A pastoral scene in Gilead. It could just as well be in the highlands west of the Jordan River; appropriately, ancient Israel was at home in both regions.

career out of being clever to his own advantage. He was "clever" in gaining the birthright and parental blessing that belonged to his older brother, Esau (Gen. 25:27–34; 27:1–41). Fleeing for his life, Jacob tried to bargain for his own safety beneath an angel-trodden ladder at Bethel: "If God will be with me and will keep me on this journey that I take, and will give me food to eat and garments to wear, and I return to my father's house in safety, then the LORD will be my God" (Gen. 28:20–21). Hardly a conversion prayer. After arriving in Harran, Jacob and his uncle Laban took turns "being clever" to each other (Gen. 29–31), and then he set his sights for home.

Traveling the same route that Abraham had decades before, Jacob followed the edge of the North Arabian Desert back to Canaan, with a large herd of grazing animals that dictated the pace of travel. Reaching the highlands of Gilead opposite what was to become the heartland of Israel, Jacob heard that Esau was coming to meet him—certainly, he reasoned, remembering the double wrong Jacob had done him and bent on revenge. Jacob tried to buy Esau off with large portions of his own herd; Esau kept on coming (Gen. 32:3–21). Then Jacob sent his entire family on ahead, across the ford of the Jabbok, willing, it seems, to turn even them over to Esau in order to ensure his own survival. Then, somewhere deep in these hills, in the dark of night and all alone, Jacob wrestled a man (so says Gen. 32:24; only much later does Hos. 12:4 identify the being as an angel). Was it Esau? One of his thugs? Not until daybreak did Jacob realize he had met God once again; this time, he was subdued. When they were finally reconciled, God changed Jacob's name to Israel: from "heel-grabber" to "one who strives with God and men, yet prevails" (Gen. 32:28). It is important to notice that God didn't change Jacob's personality—he just rearranged Jacob's convictions and priorities so that his type-A energy was now working alongside God, rather than just working for himself.

The rest of the Bible is the story of Jacob's descendants acting a whole lot like him. And so, just before their exile, when the Judeans were being hauled past the Gilead hills and up and over to Babylon, Jeremiah summed up the end game:

> *"The heart is more deceitful than all else and is desperately sick; who can understand it?"* —Jeremiah 17:9

The word "deceitful" is the verbal form of "Jacob." In other words, we are all more like Jacob than we can possibly imagine. Then the prophet continued:

> *"I, the LORD, search the heart, I test the mind, even to give to each man according to his ways, according to the results of his deeds."* —Jeremiah 17:10

So we get what we deserve, and it's not a pretty scene.

But of course gospel readers know that through the voluntary grace of Jesus, a son of Jacob who broke the pattern of what it means to be clever, a way was found that saves us from what we deserve.

38. East of Edom

The highlands of Edom south and east of the Dead Sea are not an easy place to live. The rainfall is less than half that of Jerusalem, just enough to hope for a thin crop of barley. The soils are immature and collect only here and there among the rock-strewn hills. The elevation is twice that of Jerusalem, a mile high straight up out of the Rift Valley, where the winds blow strong, winters are heavy, and spring blooms late. This was the homeland of the descendants of Esau, twin brother of Jacob, folk who lived not in the relative security of the highland folds

of Judah but out on the high desert fringe. They were a tough bunch, and understandably so.

But south and east even of Edom—now that's harsh. This landscape is known to most who visit the Hashemite Kingdom of Jordan as the high desert flats east of Petra, with barren views that do little to lift our gaze up and out through the bus window. The chalky, arid wilderness beyond Edom bleeds into Wadi Rum and the North Arabian Desert, its patches of grainy soil thinning to goat grazing land beyond where even sheep are able to go. Here precipitation is sporadic and wholly unpredictable;

The barren highlands east of Edom carry a resource base where goats, but not sheep, can survive.

Students of biblical geography—and the book of Job—learn how to pitch a Bedouin tent in the desert of Wadi Rum, beyond the land of Edom.

the yearly total can come in a single deluge, sometimes as a high desert snowfall. And then the wasteland beyond even that. Lifestyle expectations are materially meager out on this arid fringe. Prior to modern times this was the homeland of true people of the desert, semi-nomads with goat-hair tents and flocks restlessly looking for the next available water; or camel caravan traders tracking through, carrying goods from places far afield such as southern Arabia or the Persian Gulf (see Isa. 60:6–7).

It takes special skills to live in a place like this. Some of these skills are of the mind, some are of the body, some are of the heart. In our heads we have fabled pictures of gurus steeped in wisdom living in places inaccessible, high on mountains, out across deserts, hidden in caves. These images are actually biblical. "Is there no longer any wisdom in Teman?" intoned the prophet Jeremiah (49:7), mentioning a place somewhere in Edom that was renowned for its wisdom. And Obadiah called down a judgment on the homeland of the descendants of Esau that gutted one of their most renowned commodities: "Destroy wise men from Edom" (Obad. 8). The late professor of biblical theology Elmer Martens described wisdom as skill in living, an utterly practical definition. The harsher the environment, be it physical, social, or moral, the greater the need for skill.

In the biblical world, one of the possessors of skill in living was Job, who pitched his tent in this eastern desert. The narrative line of the book of Job is well known: A great sheikh lost his possessions, his family, and his own health; his friends insisted that he must have done something wrong to deserve such a fate; defending his innocence, he questioned the goodness of God. The poetry is powerful, rich, and complex, fully appropriate for the endeavor. And it is packed with geographical imagery, much of which reflects the landscape south and east of Edom. The book of Job makes great reading for visitors heading to Petra, who have an hours-long chance to gaze into the geographical setting of one of the most profound set of questions in religious literature.

Two examples: In depicting the faithlessness of his friends—the worst fate imaginable in desert culture—Job replies with geographical language that is precise to the high desert of the eastern Edomite watershed:

"My brothers have acted deceitfully like a wadi, like the torrents of wadis which vanish, which are turbid because of ice and into which the snow melts. When they become waterless, they are silent, when it is hot, they vanish from their place. The paths of their course wind along, they go up into nothing and perish." —Job 6:15–18

And Job turns inward to liken the destiny of the righteous sufferer—himself—to that of the tent dweller, which he also was. Though fragile in its material substance, the goat-hair tent provides security for everyone within, through cultural values of hospitality and protection that have developed over millennia and withstood the test of time. Yet,

"He is torn from the security of his tent. . . . There dwells in his tent nothing of his; brimstone is scattered on his habitation. His roots are dried below, and his branch is cut off above." —Job 18:14–16

The high, arid desert in Wadi Rum, south of Edom.

The book of Job resolves not with direct answers to Job's questions, but with a rhetorical response from God. Speaking from the whirlwind and using imagery from Job's own natural world (whirlwinds themselves are common out on these high, hot desert flats), the Lord declares what should have been obvious all along. Job's skills in living, as refined as they are, are wholly inadequate when compared to the infinite wisdom of God. That's all he needed to know.

> *"Have you ever in your life commanded the morning, and caused the dawn to know its place ... ?"*
>
> —Job 38:12

> *"Who has cleft a channel for the flood, or a way for the thunderbolt, to bring rain on a land without people, on a desert without a man in it ... ?"* —Job 38:25–26

> *"Who sent out the wild donkey free? And who loosed the bonds of the swift donkey, to whom I gave the wilderness for a home and the salt land for his dwelling place?"*
>
> —Job 39:5–6

And so on. Recognizing his place, Job retracts his plea and repents in dust and ashes (Job 42:6). God chose to restore Job's fortunes twofold (Job 42:10–17) and, in our sense of divine economy, all ended well. But what if it didn't? Does anything change if the book ends not with a visible return to blessing, but simply Job's acknowledgment that his own wisdom was insufficient before God's?

39. Grounded Foresight

It was, quite literally, a view for the ages. Standing on Mount Nebo at the end of his life, Moses was able to peer into the promised land, a land that God had forbidden him to enter. Scanning the horizon in a counterclockwise sweep, Moses must have been breathless with anticipation. The future of his people lay before him. This was to be their new home.

Now Moses went up from the plains of Moab to Mount Nebo, to the top of Pisgah, which is opposite Jericho. And the LORD

This view from Mount Nebo is toward the northwest, across the plains of Moab to the rise of the hills of Ephraim and Manasseh beyond.

showed him all the land, Gilead as far as Dan, and all of Naphtali and the land of Ephraim and Manasseh, and all the land of Judah as far as the western sea [the Mediterranean], and the Negev and the plain in the valley of Jericho, the city of palm trees, as far as Zoar.

—Deuteronomy 34:1–3

These verses may be a cartographer's dream, but they pose a geographical challenge. Some of the places listed—most notably the Mediterranean Sea—are

impossible to see from the traditional site of Mount Nebo, a mere bump atop the line of hills in Transjordan opposite Jericho. The highest visible point west of Mount Nebo, the Mount of Olives, blocks the line of sight for everything beyond. We are left to wonder how Moses could possibly have seen all that Deuteronomy claims he did.

Some might ask, but did he? Perhaps another site with a better view was called Mount Nebo in Moses' day. Or, maybe Moses was mistaken in what he saw, falling victim to a bout of wishful thinking. Or better yet,

The view from Mount Nebo to the west, across the Dead Sea and toward the rise of the hill country of Judah.

The Brazen Serpent monument atop Mount Nebo, created by Italian artist Giovanni Fantoni. The monument intertwines images of the serpent that Moses lifted up in the wilderness with the cross of Jesus.

perhaps we should somehow spiritualize the passage, concluding that Moses simply anticipated the extent of the promised land without actually seeing it himself.

There is no need to be geographically skeptical. While it is not possible to see the Mediterranean from today's Mount Nebo and no other hill in the area improves the view, the sea *is* visible from the higher hills of Gilead some forty miles to the north. Over 100 years ago, long before the air was clouded by industrial pollution, travelers to Gilead reported seeing the Mediterranean Sea from the lofty hills between the ruins of the crusader castle at Ajlun and those of the once-magnificent Roman city of Jerash. One such traveler was Bertha Spafford Vester, daughter of Horatio Spafford (composer of the hymn "It Is Well with My Soul"), who recorded the view in her book, *Our Jerusalem*.

How is this possible? Looking southwestward from the hills above Jerash, Bertha Vester peered over a saddle in the central hilly spine of Canaan where the Old Testament tribal inheritance of Benjamin was located (see Josh. 18:11–28). On a straight line much further southwest she spotted the seaport of Gaza, hugging the Mediterranean shore as it sweeps westward toward Egypt. Her view was improved by gazing through the brilliantly clear skies that always follow a spell of heavy winter rains in the land.

While we need not look for Mount Nebo around Ajlun and Jerash, we should remember that Moses himself had traveled through Gilead on his way to defeat Og, king of Bashan, in battle (Deut. 3:1–17). Is it unreasonable to think that he might also have seen the Mediterranean as he crossed these hills? As he gazed into the land west of the Jordan River seeking to see as much territory as he possibly could, Moses surely must have remembered the journey of the twelve spies whom he had sent into Canaan almost forty years before (see Num. 13:1–24). It does not stretch the text of Deuteronomy 34 to suggest that, as Moses peered into the promised land from Mount Nebo, God simply brought to mind all that he had *already* seen from various vantage points east of the Jordan. There is no need spiritualize the passage if we remember that Moses, the greatest of all the Old Testament prophets (Deut. 34:10–11), tended to see matters of life through spiritual eyes.

God showed Moses something of his people's future, but his view was neither abstract nor disconnected from reality. For Moses, the future was quite literally grounded in historic and geographical reality. It would be good for Christians today, we who are living at a time when many of us seem to be overly anxious about what might happen tomorrow, to remember that our future lies in the hands of a God with a perfect track record of taking care of his people in the present.

40. A Bit of Method

Signposts: Anywhere in Judea, Samaria, or Galilee

Having spent some time "reading" the lands of the Bible so that we can better "see" the text, it is perhaps a good time to ask the question, "How do we know what we know?" In particular, how do we know that our understanding of the context of the Bible is accurate, or at least reasonable, given our distance from that world (in time and likely in place)? Many of us are used to understanding the Bible through faith, and then viewing its claims, either consciously or not, first through the lens of our own lives and times. Taking the Bible by faith recognizes that it is divinely inspired and includes a good deal of

A Hebrew language scroll of the book of Ruth, a story ripe with geographical realities.

information that was known to its writers only through revelation. But viewing its stories and claims through our own life and times, with the proper goal of making it relevant to today, should be the end of a process of understanding, not the beginning.

A student of biblical geography maps events told on the pages of Scripture.

In sermons, homilies, and Sunday school lessons, teachers of the Bible tend to focus on practical theology, a way of drawing on the text to address specific questions that we are asking, or issues that we are facing, in our own day-to-day lives. Practical theology typically draws its data from systematic theology, a comprehensive attempt to understand what the entire Bible teaches about foundational topics such as creation, God, humanity, salvation, or the church. Theologians working in systematic theology base their understanding of these topics on what scholars call biblical theology, that is, what the writers of the individual books of the Bible emphasized in their own writings: the specific teachings of Isaiah for instance, or Matthew, or Paul. And these writers were fully immersed in . . . the

 Permission granted by Biblical Backgrounds, Inc. (bibback.com).

world of the Bible! "God . . . is a rock," the psalmist said (18:2, 31), a characterization that is a bit odd given that rocks are cold, inanimate objects. Somehow, the reality of the rocks that the psalmist knew has to work its way back up through the language of our biblical, systematic, and practical theologies so that their God-like qualities can impact our day-to-day lives. So how *do* we know what we know, so that we can be sure that the practical theology of today is based on truths that are truly biblical?

The process begins by recognizing the "stuff" of the world that the biblical writers were immersed in, the items that they used not only to tell us what happened, but to convey things of the heart. Geographical information fills the biblical text. The authors of the Bible naturally and quite freely used elements of geography as images to help us understand other, greater realities, such as the character of God and of ourselves.

Four bodies of data help us recognize this "stuff." The first is texts, that is, the Bible itself, but also other texts contemporary with it that provide context. We do well to read these for geographical data, knowing that the biblical authors spoke honestly and correctly about the physical world in which they lived. That world was not only their home, it was also the home of their initial audience, and they knew that their readers could easily check the reliability of the information they gave. The second body of data is geography—the lay of the land, its natural resources, its climate and living conditions.

And this is best grasped when we take time to interact with it face-to-face. When the Bible says "mountain," what does it mean? Certainly not the Rockies! When it speaks of "rain for your land in its season" (Deut. 11:14), can it be referring to summertime?

The third is archaeology, the process of uncovering the actual material culture of the world of the Bible. Here the pool of data is endless, and always growing. When properly handled, archaeological data neither proves nor disproves the Bible, but rather provides a tangible context in which the material culture mentioned in the Bible (everything from city walls to pots) can be placed. And the fourth body of data comes from historic anthropology, the study of culture now and in the past. In what ways might traditional societies of the Middle East preserve the essential values and living patterns of peoples who lived in the same regions in Bible times?

Having gathered data from these four sources, we then need to square it up to see how it points in directions that are meaningful for understanding the Bible. The process is neither easy nor quick, nor are the results necessarily obvious. But we do gain skills in setting parameters of what the biblical writers could or could not have meant, given the reality of their own living space. "X" is in bounds, for instance, while "Y" is out of bounds. In the process, we gain skills in determining if our own interpretations are found within the possibilities afforded by the biblical world, or not.

The apostle John, likely the "disciple whom Jesus loved" (John 20:2, etc.), reminded his

readers that he, and they, were eyewitnesses to things concerning their Lord:

> *What was from the beginning, what we have heard, what we have seen with our eyes, what we have looked at and touched with our hands, concerning the Word of Life . . .* —1 John 1:1

Archaeologists excavate a portion of Gezer that was destroyed by the Assyrians in the late eighth century BC.

He could have added tasted and smelled, since his own experiences with Jesus included the intimacy of long walks under the hot sun, endless waits for sunrise, meals—all the stuff of everyday life. We, too, are eyewitnesses of the context in which Jesus and the people we meet on the pages of the Bible lived when we take time to immerse ourselves into their geographical realities; when we look at (or even excavate) pieces of the material culture of their worlds; and when we get to know how the values, behaviors, and living conditions of people still living in the Middle East reflect those of people who lived here in the time of the Bible.

For twenty years my wife and I have hosted upwards of 800 students of biblical historical geography yearly at receptions in our home on Mount Zion in Jerusalem. I typically encourage them to share bullet points of what they have experienced while learning how to read the land. I have heard many insightful things over the years. Here's one: "The stories of the Bible are just the beginning. They continue today. And there are still people living in Bible places!" This budding observer of the world of the Bible saw that there is an essential connection between the ways that God met people back then and the ways that he continues to meet people today. Between their context and ours. Between the human condition then, and the human condition now.

So the story is still being told. And lived, by people like you and me.

Index of Biblical Passages Quoted

Index of Signposts

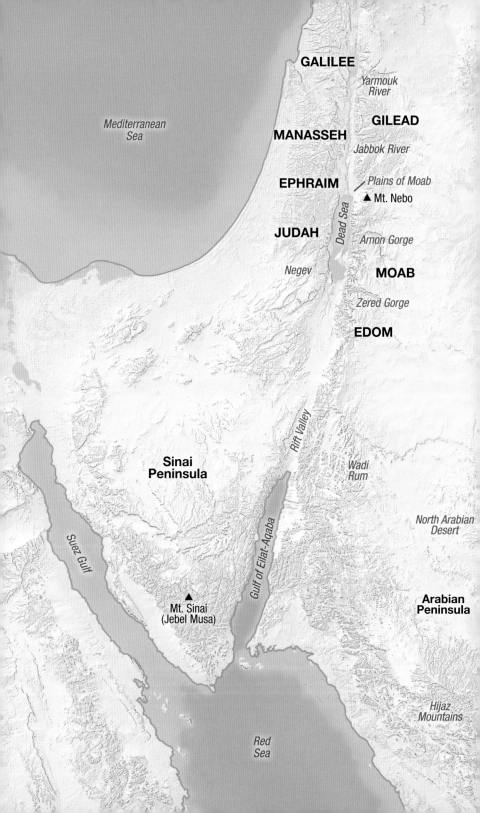

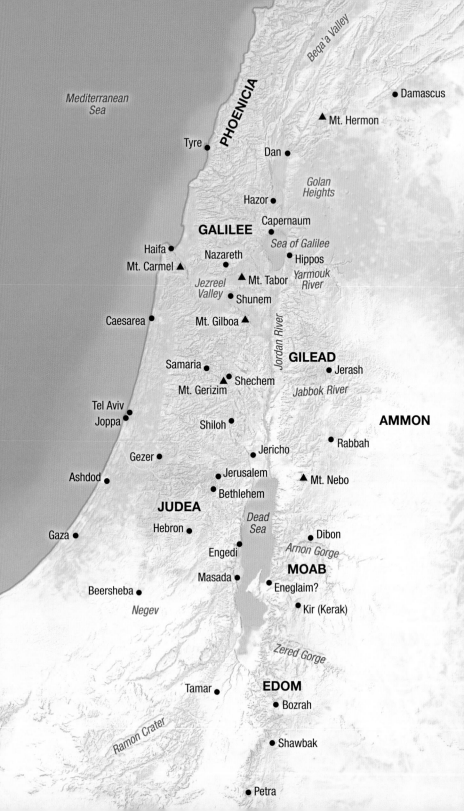

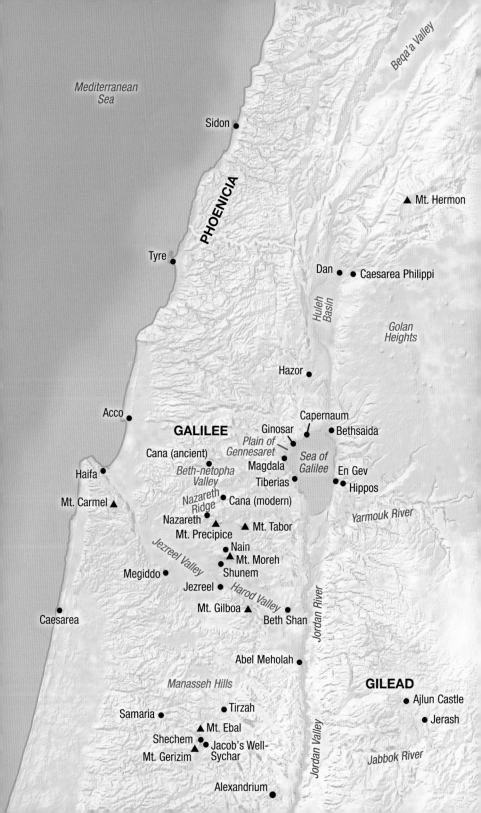

Mediterranean
Sea

Sidon

PHOENICIA

Mt. Hermon

Beqa'a Valley

Tyre

Dan • Caesarea Philippi

Huleh
Basin

Golan
Heights

Hazor

Acco

GALILEE

Capernaum

Ginosar • Bethsaida

Cana (ancient)

Plain of
Gennesaret

Sea of
Galilee

Haifa

Beth-netopha
Valley

Magdala

Tiberias

En Gev
Hippos

Mt. Carmel

Nazareth
Ridge

Cana (modern)

Yarmouk River

Nazareth

Mt. Tabor

Mt. Precipice

Nain

Jezreel Valley

Mt. Moreh

Shunem

Megiddo

Jezreel

Harod Valley

Mt. Gilboa

Beth Shan

Jordan River

Caesarea

Abel Meholah

Manasseh Hills

GILEAD

Tirzah

Ajlun Castle

Samaria

Jerash

Mt. Ebal

Shechem

Jacob's Well-
Sychar

Mt. Gerizim

Jordan Valley

Jabbok River

Alexandrium

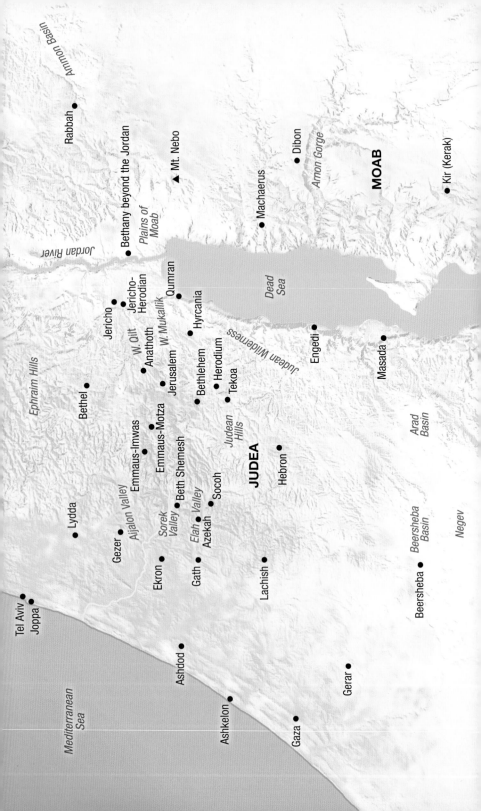

Sanhedria

Ammunition Hill

Hebrew University ■

Mount Scopus ▲

Haim Bar-Lev Ave.

Glick Observation Plaza

Nablus Road

Mea Shearim

EAST JERUSALEM

WEST JERUSALEM

Augusta Victoria Compound

Saint-Étienne Monastery

Garden of Gethsemane & Church of All Nations

Jaffa Road

Garden Tomb ■

Church of Mary Magdalene

Sacher Park

Zion Square ■

Church of the Ascension

Ben-Zvi Ave.

King George V St.

Safra Square ■

Old City

Mount of Olives ▲

Agron St.

Absalom's Pillar ■

Rehavia

Kidron Valley

City of David ■

Israel Museum

Pool of Siloam

Mount Zion ▲

Silwan

Valley of the Son of Hinnom

Abu Tor

Emeq Rephaim

Baq'a

Jebel Mukabir

Bethlehem Road

Hebron Road

Daniel Yanovski St

Government House

Talpiot

■ Versailles Wedding Hall Memorial

East Talpiot

The Old City of Jerusalem

HEROD'S GATE

DAMASCUS GATE

Pool of Bethesda

MUSLIM QUARTER

LION'S / ST. STEPHEN'S GATE

NEW GATE

Via Dolorosa

Church of the Holy Sepulchre

Haram al-Sharif / Temple Mount

Khan Ez-Zeit Street

Central (Tyropoean) Valley

El- Wad Street

CHRISTIAN QUARTER

David Street

Western (Wailing) Wall

Mount Zion (biblical)

JAFFA GATE

Western Wall plaza

ARMENIAN QUARTER

JEWISH QUARTER

Habad Street

DUNG GATE

Church of St. James

ZION GATE

Rev. Dr. Paul H. Wright is President of Jerusalem University College / Institute of Holy Land Studies, located on Mount Zion in Jerusalem. For twenty-five years he has taught biblical geography, on site, to thousands of college-age and adult students.

Paul's journey traces a path from the table-flat lands of Illinois to the rugged terrain of the hill country of Judah. For generations, his family roots have been in farming and teaching, analogous endeavors. Planting, tending, growth, harvest, seed that produces seed that produces seed—it's an ongoing process in the classroom and in the field. He believes that teaching, writing, and fieldwork are crafts much like woodworking, which he also enjoys—all require a measure of patience, an eye for detail, and a willingness to get one's hands dirty in the process of creating something useful. His wife, Diane, has shared this walk for nearly forty years (and counting). For the last twenty, Paul and Diane have shared leadership roles at Jerusalem University College, living literally on the foundations of the wall that surrounded the city during part of the Old (and all of the New) Testament. By growing up in Jerusalem, their two children gained assets that allowed them to raise their own families in ways that are intentionally open and caring.

Paul received his PhD at Hebrew Union College, Cincinnati, Ohio, and an MA in Old Testament from Trinity Evangelical Divinity School, Deerfield, Illinois.

Image Credits

Photo on pages 32–33 used by permission of Tan Eng Boo. Photos on pages 35, 64, 129, 160, and 236 used by permission of Tiffany Gibson. Photo on page 132 used by permission of Diane Wright. Photo on page 203 used by permission of Tim Wright. Photo on pages 230–31 used by permission of Lawson Stone. All other photos used by permission of Paul H. Wright.

Cover photo: John Theodor/Shutterstock.com